The Attitude Advantage

Rosemary T. Fruehling, Ph.D.

Roberta Moore

Teacher materials follow the student text.

Publisher
The Goodheart-Willcox Company, Inc.
Tinley Park, Illinois
www.g-w.com

Library of Congress Cataloging-in-Publication Data
Fruehling, Rosemary T.
    The attitude advantage / Rosemary T. Fruehling, Roberta Moore.
    p. cm.
    ISBN 978-1-59070-855-2
    1. High school graduates--Employment--United States. 2. High
school students--Employment--United States. 3. Interpersonal relations--
United States. 4. Vocational guidance--United States. I. Moore, Roberta
II. Title.
HD6273.F78 2008
650.1'3--dc22   2007022473

Portions of this work were previously published as *Your Attitude Counts*, by
Rosemary T. Fruehling and Neild B. Oldham, by Paradigm Publishing, Inc.

To the Teacher

The *Teacher's Annotated Edition* of *The Attitude Advantage* is designed to make the teaching experience easy for you and the learning experience fun for your students. The complete student text follows, with answers in red for all the discussion questions and review questions. This format gives you the answers right where you need them—in the student text.

At the back of the student text are *The Attitude Advantage* teacher materials. This section provides
* articles on teaching strategies
* topic overviews
* reproducible masters for self-assessments and activities

All these items are designed to help you teach students how to develop a constructive attitude and apply human relations skills at work, at school, and in all other areas of life.

To the Student

One of the most important factors in your success is your ability to get along with others. This ability is called *human relations skills*. A person's human relations skills are a reflection of his or her attitudes. If your attitude is positive and constructive, you will have a great advantage in work and in life.

The Attitude Advantage is designed to introduce you to human relations skills and teach you the most important skills in a fun, easy-to-read format. The book consists of 22 topics organized into four parts.

Part 1 introduces you to human relations skills and attitudes and describes the different kinds of relationships that exist at work. Part 2 analyzes constructive and destructive attitudes at work and shows their impact on morale and productivity. Part 3 focuses on how to build good interpersonal relationships. Part 4 presents ways to learn from mistakes and repair damaged relationships. The final topic looks at positive ways to leave a job.

Each topic is organized into four sections. The first section is "Discover." It includes objectives for the topic and a case study that illustrates the topic. The second section is "Analyze." This section discusses the key concepts of the topic and how the case illustrates them. Key terms in the "Analyze" section are highlighted in bold and defined in the glossary at the end of the book.

The third section is "Apply." This section provides another case to which you can apply the concepts you learned in the "Analyze" section. The last section, "Review," gives you an opportunity to review what you have learned by answering some questions. Throughout each topic are "Discuss" sections. These sections pose thought-provoking questions about the cases and the topic.

This book was designed to help you learn how to interact positively with others and to achieve success through a positive, constructive attitude.

About the Authors

Rosemary T. Fruehling received her B.S., M.A., and Ph.D. degrees from the University of Minnesota in Minneapolis. She has taught office education at both the high school and postsecondary levels and has conducted business education teacher-training. She was the manager of postsecondary vocational education for the Minnesota State Department of Education and director of software technology development for the State of Minnesota. Rosemary has served as a consultant to many businesses and has authored several business textbooks.

Roberta Moore received her B.A. from Wayne State University in Detroit, Michigan. She has comprehensive experience in trade, professional, and educational publishing. She was an editor and manager of vocational and business education publishing programs with McGraw-Hill and has worked as a consultant for other major publishers. Roberta has authored several business textbooks. She currently runs her own consulting business in publishing, marketing, and communications.

Contents

Part 3
Succeeding on the Job 76

Part 4
Dealing with Problems on the Job 122

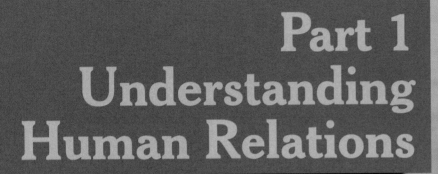

Part 1
Understanding
Human Relations

The Need for Human Relations Skills

DISCOVER

- what human relations is.
- why you need human relations skills.
- how human relations skills help you on the job.

Case: Who Is the Best Candidate?

In a large high school, Bethany and Natasha are running for president of their junior class. The class sponsors two important events: homecoming and the junior-senior spring dance. The class needs to elect a strong, capable leader to make these events a success. The class president must be able to work well with others. She also must be a good organizer, able to assign tasks to others. She will need to set up schedules to get the work done on time. As the leader, she also needs to let people be creative so working on the events will be fun.

Your success is influenced by how well you relate to others.

DISCUSS

1. What is your reaction to this case?

   Sample responses: I don't think Natasha will be a good president; why did they vote for her? Natasha is the right person because everyone liked her better. Bethany ran a better campaign; she should have won.

2. Which candidate would you vote for? Why?

   Sample responses: I would vote for Bethany because she has student council experience and is more organized. I would vote for Natasha because she is a hard worker and better with people.

Bethany is a strong candidate. She is on the student council and has organized many student events. She is an honor student, and her teachers and her peers like her. They know she is capable, serious, and smart. Bethany is sure of herself. She is eager to show that she can be a good leader.

Natasha is a hard worker. She gets good grades. She is active in sports and does volunteer work in her community. She loves being with people and has a lot of friends. Natasha's teachers think her behavior always reflects her drive to be good at what she does.

The campaigns of the two candidates are quite different. Bethany is cool and confident. She campaigns on her skills. Her posters list her experience as a leader and a problem-solver. She also creates a Web site and holds question-and-answer sessions online. This way she is sure not to fall behind in her studies. A student asks what she will do if one of her project leaders falls behind on his or her tasks. Bethany says that she will make the tough decision.

She will replace the person with someone who can get the work done. There is no question that Bethany is capable of making the two junior class functions a success.

Natasha is warm and open-minded. She makes a point of talking to as many classmates as possible during the school day. She doesn't say much about how she will handle her job as class president. She focuses on asking for ideas and listening to what people have to say about the two junior class events. She assures her peers that what they tell her is important. When asked what she will do if one of her project leaders isn't getting the job done, Natasha says she will talk to the person and find out why. She will try her best to help everyone succeed. The day before the election, she talks to and sends e-mails and text messages to as many people as she can. She asks for their support and the support of their friends.

Bethany and Natasha are both qualified for the job. However, when it comes to solid skills for organizing the events, Bethany is the best choice. The junior class elects Natasha.

ANALYZE

You can have excellent job skills and still fail to achieve your career goals. You can also be honest and hard working, but even that does not guarantee success. Why? The reason is that almost everything you do is affected by how well you relate to people. When you **interact** with other people, you are engaged in **human relations**. Human relations skills are a key factor in the success of most people. In work and all aspects of life, you cannot escape interacting with people, nor would you want to. **Human relations skills** are the skills you use to make your interactions with people as positive as possible.

Why You Need Good Human Relations Skills

In a single day, you interact with many people. You interact with classmates, friends, teachers, and others in school. You may interact with salespeople, bus drivers, and others in your neighborhood. At times, you may not be aware of how others see you or how they feel about your behavior. At other times, you go out of your way to make a good impression. There are even times when you don't care what others think about you. No matter what you are thinking, how you relate to others affects everything that happens to you.

The study of human relations helps you understand why people behave the way they do. You will see why they think and feel the way they do. The study of human relations will also help you learn more about yourself. As you learn more about yourself, you will be able to adjust your behavior to improve your interaction with others.

Human Relations Is Communicating

Interaction between people involves **communication**. Communication is sending messages from one person to another. Communication involves talking, listening, writing, and reading. Communication is the essence of human relations.

Communication can be verbal or nonverbal.

Verbal communication is communication using words. The impact and clarity of communication depends on the words you choose. Whether others "get" your message depends on whether they understand your words and how they interpret your words.

Nonverbal communication is communication without words. How can you communicate without words? Think of waving hello to a friend. Nonverbal communication includes gestures, facial expressions, and actions. Nonverbal communication is also called **body language**.

Even what you wear and how you walk communicate messages to others. Clothing and posture are part of nonverbal communication. For example, around your peers, your jeans and T-shirt say, "I'm part of the crowd." On a job interview at a corporate office, the same clothes would communicate a different message. Regardless of what you wanted to say, in this setting the message would be, "I don't fit in here."

Human Relations Is an Essential Job Skill

If you focus, as Bethany did, on work skills alone, you may find it much harder to succeed at work. On the other hand, you will probably have a hard time if you have no work skills, even if you are very charming. People who are all charm often manage to get others to do their work. In this way, the charmer may appear successful. Such a person is an example of the power of good human relations skills. Usually,

the charmer's lack of skills is ultimately discovered.

For your best chance at success, develop your work skills and your human relations skills. Natasha had the work skills needed for the job. She also realized that an important part of her campaign, and an important part of being president, is interacting with people. She focused her campaign on interacting with people and won.

Good Human Relations Requires Self-Awareness

At times, you are aware of what you are communicating to others. At other times, you are not. Being aware of how you communicate is an important step in developing good human relations skills. The next step is being aware of how people react to you. The combination of being aware of yourself *and* the reactions of others is called **self-awareness**. Being aware of yourself does *not* mean that you should constantly worry about what others think of you. It does mean that you need to think about how your actions are received by others.

Once you have self-awareness, you can develop skills to improve your communication. You can more consciously speak and act in ways that have a positive effect on people. The goal of good human relations skills is to have positive and constructive relationships. The cases in this book will help you achieve this goal.

DISCUSS

1. Which candidate would you vote for? Why?
   Sample responses: I would still vote for Bethany because she has student council experience and is more organized. I would change my vote to Natasha because she is better with people.

2. Why did the class elect Natasha?
   Sample response: Natasha's campaign focused on connecting with students and listening to their ideas.

3. Do you think Natasha will be successful? Give your reasons.
   Sample responses: Yes, she will be able to develop a good team of students to work on the events. No, she is not organized or experienced enough.

4. What advice would you give to Bethany?
   Sample response: Ask others for their opinions and listen to them.

5. What could Natasha learn from Bethany?
   Sample response: Sometimes leaders have to make tough decisions and replace someone who is not following through.

APPLY

Case:
Employee Personalities

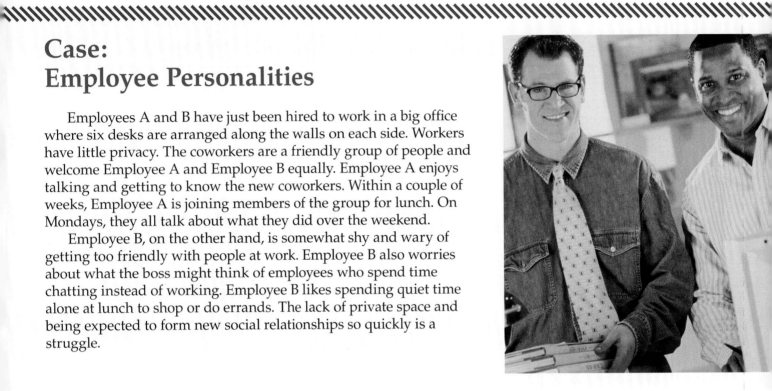

Employees A and B have just been hired to work in a big office where six desks are arranged along the walls on each side. Workers have little privacy. The coworkers are a friendly group of people and welcome Employee A and Employee B equally. Employee A enjoys talking and getting to know the new coworkers. Within a couple of weeks, Employee A is joining members of the group for lunch. On Mondays, they all talk about what they did over the weekend.

Employee B, on the other hand, is somewhat shy and wary of getting too friendly with people at work. Employee B also worries about what the boss might think of employees who spend time chatting instead of working. Employee B likes spending quiet time alone at lunch to shop or do errands. The lack of private space and being expected to form new social relationships so quickly is a struggle.

DISCUSS

1. What are the advantages of being like Employee A?
   Sample response: You get to know everyone you work with.

2. What are the advantages of being like Employee B?
   Sample response: You focus more on your work than on your coworkers.

3. What are the drawbacks of being like Employee A?
   Sample response: You might socialize too much and neglect your work.

4. What are the drawbacks of being like Employee B?
   Sample response: You might not have good working relationships with your coworkers.

5. At work, how much socializing is too much?
   Sample response: Too much socializing at work occurs when you socialize instead of doing your work or socialize so long that you are late returning from lunch and breaks.

REVIEW

True or False

Circle *T* if the statement is true or *F* if the statement is false.

(T) F   1. Almost everything people do in life is affected by how they relate to others.

T (F)   2. Human relations involves only the positive interactions with others.

(T) F   3. Communication is the essence of human relations.

T (F)   4. *Verbal communication* is another term for *body language*.

T (F)   5. Nonverbal communication includes the words a person says to others.

(T) F   6. Being aware of oneself as well as the reactions of others is called self-awareness.

(T) F   7. Self-awareness is a necessary part of good human relations.

T (F)   8. People with excellent work skills do *not* need good human relation skills.

T (F)   9. People can achieve success on the job without work skills if they have good human relations skills.

(T) F   10. The goal of human relations is to have positive and constructive relationships.

Check Your Understanding

1. Describe two different kinds of communication.
   Verbal communication uses words. Nonverbal communication is communication without words.

2. How can self-awareness help you improve your human relations skills?
   If you know how others react to your behavior, you can change your behavior to get a better response.

3. How do human relations skills help you on the job?
   Good human relations skills make your interactions with people on the job pleasant and productive.

4. Why are human relations skills important for your future?
   If you have good human relations skills, you will be more productive and people will probably like you. As a result, you are more likely to advance in your career.

Your Attitude Counts

DISCOVER

- the difference between a positive attitude and a negative one.
- how attitude affects behavior.
- how attitudes can change.

Case: Who Has a Positive Attitude?

Carlos is a senior in high school and cocaptain of the soccer team. He has many friends and being popular is important to him. He is looking forward to going away to college next year. He hopes to join the college soccer team. Carlos plans to work hard and do well in school and in his career.

After the big homecoming game, Carlos is invited to a party at Jason's home. Jason has spread the word that his parents are out of town, and he has invited everybody. Carlos doesn't know Jason very well, but he has heard that Jason gives fun parties. However, the fact that no adults

Your behavior is influenced by your attitude.

will be there makes Carlos nervous. He asks Nick, his best friend and team cocaptain, what they should do. Nick says, "Are you kidding? Of course we should go. The best parties are the ones without parents!"

When Carlos and Nick arrive at the party, they find lots of people and loud music. Carlos is having a great time, until he sees three boys carrying cases of beer into the kitchen. "I'm getting out of here," he says to himself. He knows that if his coach finds out that he was at a beer party, he will be kicked off the team. He tells Nick they should go, but Nick says, "Hey, man, no harm, no foul." Nick explains that if they don't drink anything, it's okay to stay.

About an hour later, the doorbell rings. Two police officers enter the house. A neighbor called to report underage kids drinking beer and acting wild. The police see open beer cans and ask the teens for their IDs. All are underage, and the police give each an underage drinking ticket. They all must attend a three-hour course on underage drinking and pay $20 to cover its cost.

Nick says, "Don't tell the coach about it. We didn't drink any beer, so why tell him?" However, Carlos decides to tell his parents and his coach. He's afraid they will find out anyway. The coach gives Carlos another chance, and his parents believe his explanation. Carlos tells them that he will be more careful about the parties he goes to.

When Carlos attends the course, he listens and participates in the discussions. He leaves knowing that he has learned how to handle situations involving alcohol. Carlos is glad to have this knowledge before going off to college.

Nick, on the other hand, is resentful. He feels unfairly forced to go to the underage-drinking course because he was *not* drinking at the party. Besides, he thinks underage drinking is okay, as long as you don't get drunk.

Nick attends the course but sits in the back. While the group talks, he plays games on his cell phone. He avoids talking to anyone. Nick thinks the course is a waste of time. He is worried about what will happen if his parents or the coach find out about the party.

DISCUSS

1. What is your reaction to this case?
   Sample responses: Those guys are stupid; they never should have gone to the party in the first place. Carlos is stupid for telling his parents. I think Carlos did the right thing. I think Nick is risking his future.

2. Describe Carlos's attitude about getting the ticket.
   Carlos is concerned and worried about its impact on his life and his future.

3. Describe Nick's attitude about getting the ticket.
   Nick thinks it's no big deal as long as no one else finds out.

4. What would you have done if you were faced with the same situation?
   Sample responses: I would tell my parents, as Carlos did. I would try to hide the incident, as Nick did.

ANALYZE

An **attitude** is a belief or feeling that causes you to act in a certain way. You may have a specific attitude about a person, situation, or idea. You may have a general attitude about life. Your attitudes often affect your behavior toward others. Some attitudes are weak and easy to change. Others are strongly held and very hard to change.

Attitudes Are Learned

Where do attitudes come from? Attitudes are usually developed over the years. You learn attitudes from family and friends, the media and school. Your community and cultural background also influence your attitudes. You process all your experiences, and the results are your attitudes. These attitudes are reflected in your personality and behavior. Whether your attitudes are positive or negative depends on what you experience and learn and how you react to that.

Attitudes Can Be Positive or Negative

People with a **positive attitude** look on the bright side of situations and people. They are optimistic. When problems occur, they do not blame others. They take action to make things better. People with positive attitudes are usually happy and enjoy making others happy.

People with a **negative attitude** look on the dark side of situations and people. They are pessimistic. When problems occur, they blame others. They feel that they cannot do anything to make things better. People with negative attitudes are usually angry or sad. They often don't even notice other people.

A positive attitude makes learning and changing easier. Carlos went to the party to have fun. He made a mistake in staying at the party when the others started drinking alcohol. However, he was open-minded and willing to learn from his mistake. As a result, he will be able to make better decisions in the future. His positive attitude also had a positive influence on the others in the course.

On the other hand, a negative attitude can cause problems in getting along with people and can interfere with learning. Nick also went to the party to enjoy himself. He did not think it was a mistake to stay at the party after the drinking started. When the police gave him a ticket for underage drinking, he felt unjustly punished. He did not think he was wrong. His attitude toward the police and the course on underage drinking was negative. He was close-minded and unwilling to learn. He ignored the course, which cut him off from new experiences and new people. He did not learn any new ideas that could be useful to him in the future.

Attitudes Reflect Values

Your attitudes reflect your values. If you see yourself as an honest person, you will reject attitudes that allow cheating and stealing. If you see yourself as a victim, you may expect the worst to happen to you. You may develop an attitude that views cheating and stealing as okay because life is unfair.

Attitudes Can Change

Attitudes are learned, but they are not carved in stone. It's true that you cannot change your parents or your experiences, but you can change your attitudes. You have the power to choose which attitudes to accept and which to reject. You can change your attitudes to match the kind of person you want to be.

Think about the kind of person you want to be. Pay attention to how people respond to your words and actions. These observations can help you evaluate your choices and the attitudes behind them. Your evaluations can help you decide which attitudes you want to keep and which you want to change.

Education can lead to changes in attitude. Some negative attitudes are based on lack of information. Learning new information can change negative attitudes into positive attitudes. Reading novels, biographies, and psychology texts shows you how other people think. As you learn more, you begin to understand different points of view. Your mind opens to new ideas, and your attitudes may change.

The simple fact of maturing and having new life experiences can lead to changes in attitude. As a teenager, you may vow that you will never give your child an early curfew or take the car keys away because of poor grades. When you marry and have your own children, your attitude is likely to change. Instead of being the teen, you will be the parent worrying about your child's safety and well-being. Your new point of view may cause you to realize that your parents were not being too harsh. They were enforcing limits that were in your best interests.

Attitudes Vary

Today's workforce consists of a diverse mix of people. You may find yourself working with people from different races, cultures, and religious backgrounds. You may work with people of all ages. Your coworkers may come from a variety of economic backgrounds. They might have widely different experiences, opinions, and attitudes. Human relations skills are essential in this type of workplace. In order to work together productively, people must cooperate in spite of their differences.

Adopt the attitude that differences present opportunities. People do not need to think or act alike to do a good job. Different opinions can lead to creativity and better problem solving.

Attitudes Show

Many supervisors are skilled in reading the attitudes of their employees. You show your attitude in many ways:

- in your approach to school or a job
- in your willingness to follow directions
- in the way you handle problems
- in your reaction to criticism
- in the way you relate to coworkers
- in the way you relate to people in authority

Attitudes Can Be Contagious

A positive attitude makes human relations much easier. It can be good for your career and your personal life. How? Positive attitudes can be contagious. People often respond to a positive attitude by becoming positive themselves.

Which classes do you most enjoy? Usually, they are the classes in which the teacher is enthusiastic about the subject and about teaching. When the teacher communicates a positive attitude, students are likely to respond positively.

In your own life, which people are you most eager to see? Are you eager to see people with a positive attitude, full of fun and ideas? Do you want to spend time with people who have a negative attitude and are always complaining and discouraged? When you are negative, people tend to respond in the same way.

It's worthwhile to try to always have a positive attitude in your work environment. Even though a positive attitude may be hard to maintain, it will have a positive impact on your career. If you are energetic, motivated, productive, alert, and friendly, your coworkers and supervisors will respond positively to you. A positive attitude also will be transmitted to clients and customers.

A worker with a negative attitude can drain energy from a work group. Coworkers and customers are likely to avoid him or her. The worker with a negative attitude may be unable to work well with others. The supervisor may see the negative person as a less valuable employee.

A negative attitude can spread through a group, so workers must be careful not to develop a negative group mentality. For example, when workers fall into the habit of constantly complaining to each other about what they don't like on the job, the whole group becomes negative. Productivity and the quality of customer service may fall. Gossiping about coworkers and supervisors is another way that negative attitudes spread in the workplace.

DISCUSS

1. What choices did Carlos and Nick have *after* the police arrived at the party?
   Sample responses: They could have tried to convince the police not to give them a ticket. They could have skipped the course and gotten into more trouble. They could have decided to tell or not to tell their parents and coach.

2. How does Carlos's decision reflect his attitude and values?
   Carlos wants to succeed, and he knows that being a liar will interfere more with his success than being honest.

3. How does Nick's decision reflect his attitude and values?
   Nick believes in having fun and getting away with whatever he can.

4. Was Nick smart to keep his mouth shut?
   Sample responses: Yes, because if the coach never finds out, Nick will not get kicked off the team. No, because if the coach finds out and Nick didn't tell him or lied about it, Nick will surely be kicked off the team.

APPLY

Case: A New Coworker

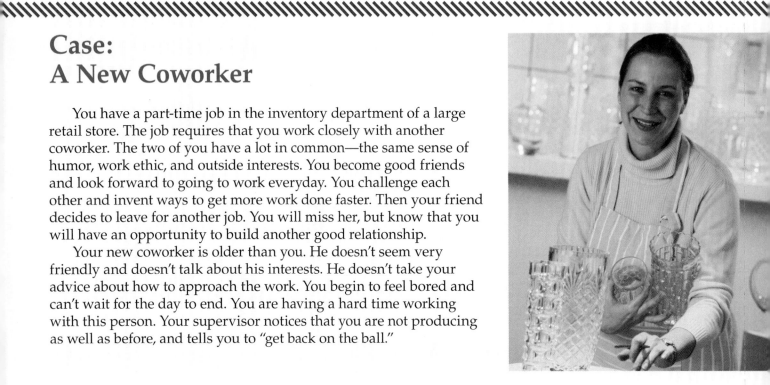

You have a part-time job in the inventory department of a large retail store. The job requires that you work closely with another coworker. The two of you have a lot in common—the same sense of humor, work ethic, and outside interests. You become good friends and look forward to going to work everyday. You challenge each other and invent ways to get more work done faster. Then your friend decides to leave for another job. You will miss her, but know that you will have an opportunity to build another good relationship.

Your new coworker is older than you. He doesn't seem very friendly and doesn't talk about his interests. He doesn't take your advice about how to approach the work. You begin to feel bored and can't wait for the day to end. You are having a hard time working with this person. Your supervisor notices that you are not producing as well as before, and tells you to "get back on the ball."

DISCUSS

1. List three options for dealing with your job situation.

   Option 1: __Sample response: Discuss the problem with the coworker.__

   Option 2: __Sample response: Complain to your supervisor about your coworker.__

   Option 3: __Sample response: Accept the fact that you will not be friends and work on developing a good work relationship.__

2. List the option you would choose, and explain why you would choose it.
   __Sample response: Option 3. Discussing the problem with the coworker may not solve the problem, which is that you do not like this person. It is not appropriate or professional to complain about a coworker to the supervisor. So you will accept the fact that you will not be friends and work on developing a good work relationship. At work, it is more important to have a good, productive working relationship than to be friends.__

REVIEW

True or False

Circle *T* if the statement is true or *F* if the statement is false.

(T) F 1. Attitude affects how a person interacts with others.

T (F) 2. Attitudes are always strongly held.

T (F) 3. Positive attitudes make it harder to learn new concepts.

(T) F 4. A person can make a decision to change his or her attitude about something.

T (F) 5. Attitudes are formed at birth and are unchanging.

T (F) 6. Although education is important, it has little effect on attitude.

(T) F 7. Lack of information can cause a person to form a negative attitude.

T (F) 8. The diversity in the workforce today makes human relations skills less important.

(T) F 9. Supervisors and coworkers can read a person's attitude in his or her behavior.

(T) F 10. A positive attitude is contagious.

Check Your Understanding

1. Explain how attitudes develop.
   <u>**Attitudes are learned from family, friends, the media, school, and experiences.**</u>

2. Describe a person with a positive attitude.
   <u>**A person with a positive attitude is happy and looks on the bright side of situations.**</u>

3. Describe a person with a negative attitude.
   <u>**A person with a negative attitude is sad or angry and looks on the dark side of situations.**</u>

4. Give an example of how an attitude affects behavior.
   <u>**Sample response: Suppose someone asks you a question. If you have a positive attitude, you might respond with a smile and a pleasant voice. If you have a negative attitude, you might respond by yelling at the person or being rude.**</u>

5. Give an example that shows how attitudes can change.
   <u>**Sample response: When a person is young, he or she may think his or her parents are too strict. However, when that person becomes a parent, he or she realizes that the parents were not being too strict. The new parent's attitude may be very similar to the attitude that the person rejected when younger.**</u>

Topic 3

Teamwork

DISCOVER

- the value of teamwork in the workplace.
- the human relations skill of cooperation.
- how a good attitude can improve teamwork.

Case: Why Did the Team Improve?

Shalita is both excited and nervous as she reports for the first day of her part-time job. She is looking forward to college in six months and needs to save money. Shalita's job is stock clerk at a local supermarket. She will be working two hours a day after school and all day Saturday.

Shalita catches on quickly to what she is supposed to do. When she arrives, she checks the computer to find out which products need restocking. She has to organize her time to get the work done during the shift. Shalita likes her job. She is dependable. She arrives on time and does the assigned work efficiently. She is friendly and

When people work well together, everyone profits.

DISCUSS

1. What is your reaction to this case?
   Sample responses: Shalita had a good influence on the others. Michael and Jessica had it easy before Shalita started.

2. Describe Shalita's attitude toward her job.
   Shalita's attitude is positive and constructive.

3. How did Shalita's work habits affect her team?
   The team observed Shalita's excellent work habits and began to imitate them.

4. What might have happened if Shalita had focused only on her own work?
   The team might not have improved.

outgoing. She likes people, and they respond to that. One of the things she likes best about her job is getting to know her coworkers.

Shalita works in the frozen food department with Michael and Jessica. Shalita always greets her coworkers pleasantly, and then goes right to work. Shalita notices that her coworkers spend up to half an hour talking before getting down to work. Sometimes, they take long breaks. Michael and Jessica don't seem to mind when work is not finished at the end of their shift. However, it bothers Shalita to see empty shelves. She works hard to complete the tasks assigned to her. She knows how important it is to the shoppers and the store managers to have well-stocked grocery shelves.

Shalita feels uncomfortable when she is idle. When her work is done early, she helps Michael and Jessica finish their tasks. Michael and Jessica are grateful for the extra help. They like Shalita a lot—she is always cheerful. Even when she's had a bad day at school, she does not let it affect her attitude at work. They notice that Shalita hasn't complained about their work habits. They begin to feel a little funny that Shalita is always helping them out. They don't discuss this, but both of them begin giving a little extra effort. There are even days when they are done early enough to help Shalita.

Their supervisor notices that the frozen food section is always the most well-stocked part of the store. He tells the workers how pleased he is with their productivity. They all get good reviews and a raise in their hourly pay. Newly hired stock clerks are sent to train with them. After three months, Shalita, Michael, and Jessica are promoted to head stock workers in three separate areas of the store.

ANALYZE

Organizations have goals they need to achieve. That's the way they stay in business. An auto company needs to make quality cars to attract sales. A police department must make the community safe for its citizens. A grocery store must have stocked shelves for its customers.

Employers want workers who help them achieve their goals. Usually, people must work together to achieve these goals. Working together can be hard. When people get along and help each other get the work done, everyone profits.

Teamwork Increases Productivity

A successful organization is like a well-oiled machine. All of its parts work together smoothly. Work teams are common in business. A **team** is a group of people who work together for a common goal. **Teamwork** is people working together to produce results. The team is responsible for getting the work done. The members of successful teams work together smoothly.

Output is the result of labor, for example, the products made by a factory. **Productivity** is a measure of output. Productivity is usually measured by the amount of work done within a given period of time. The goal of most businesses is to produce the greatest output at the lowest cost in the shortest amount of time without sacrificing quality.

Employees who get their own work done efficiently are valued. Those who are willing to help others are even more valuable. Working together increases the productivity of everyone. High productivity is the goal of most work groups.

Team Players Help the Team

Shalita is a **team player**—a worker whose actions help the team. In a team, everyone is responsible for the success of

the team. Teams are successful when each individual works to full capacity. To be most successful, the members of the team must also work well together and help each other achieve goals.

Shalita is practicing an important human relations skill: cooperation. **Cooperation** consists of working together for the common good. It is the key to good teamwork. Cooperation among group members increases productivity in many ways.

Group members
- share information.
- help each other solve problems.
- work together to improve quality and reduce errors.
- motivate each other to work smarter.
- inspire each other to come up with better ideas.

Shalita could have done her job differently. She could have adopted the attitude that she was better than the other workers. Instead of helping Michael and Jessica, she could have pointed out to her supervisor how well stocked her own area was. Shalita's personal productivity would have been high, but the productivity of her group would not have increased. Michael and Jessica would probably have started to resent Shalita. Their attitude toward their work might have become negative. As a result, their productivity would have decreased. The frozen food department would not have been a pleasant place to work!

Individual Talents Create Strong Teams

As a member of a work team, you will find that your fellow workers have different talents and skills. Some workers have great writing skills. Others are good with facts and figures. Some people see the big picture. Others focus more on details. Some are very quick, while others need more time. By working in a team, each team member contributes his or her strengths to the whole team. In this way, the team is stronger and has more talent than each individual alone has.

Even if you work mostly by yourself, being a team player will be necessary to your success. Even if you have your own individual job tasks, like Shalita did, you are still part of the overall work team. Your level of productivity may be different from your coworkers'. The important thing is to always do your best and be a team player.

DISCUSS

1. How would you describe Michael and Jessica's attitude toward their work before Shalita was hired?
They were not very serious about their work and were inefficient.
2. What might have happened to Michael and Jessica if Shalita had never been hired?
They might have continued to be inefficient. They might have gotten fired.
3. What specific actions did Shalita take to improve the productivity of her team?
She helped her coworkers when she finished early. She was pleasant and positive.
4. Suppose Shalita had never been hired, and you were the manager of Michael and Jessica. What would you have done to help them be a more productive team?
Sample response: I would have reminded them to get to work right away and get back from breaks on time. I would also have given them specific goals for each work period and given them guidance on how to meet those goals.

APPLY

Case: How to Get Ahead

You are the newest person to join the sales and customer service team at a local retail store. The store sells previously owned CDs and DVDs. Your three coworkers have been working there for several years. You want to learn the job as quickly as possible. You hope your supervisor will notice your skills and potential. By the second week on the job, you realize that your group's productivity is low. Often, while you're helping a customer, you see other customers looking around for help. Your coworkers are nowhere to be found. Customers often leave without buying. Some complain of slow service. You see that you can easily outperform your coworkers.

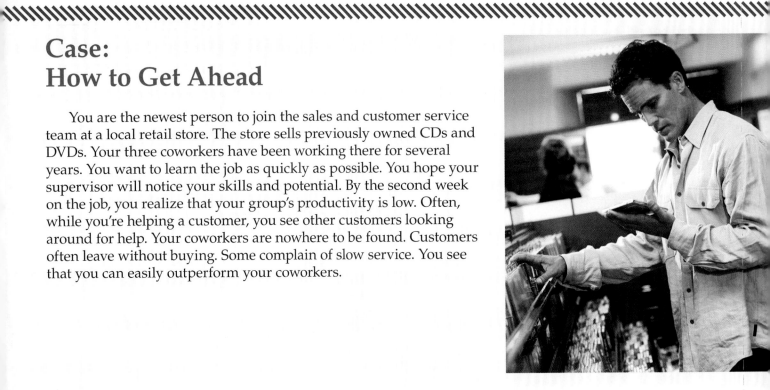

DISCUSS

1. List two options for dealing with your job situation.
   Option 1: **Sample response: Focus on your own productivity and be as productive as possible to make up for your coworkers.**
   Option 2: **Sample response: Work to increase your productivity. At the same time, develop good relationships with your coworkers, and help them with their work in a positive way.**

2. List the option you would choose, and explain why you would choose it.
   Sample response: Option 2. It's always advisable to focus on doing the best you can at your job. At the same time, good relationships with coworkers often lead to increased productivity for the whole group.

REVIEW

True or False

Circle T if the statement is true or F if the statement is false.

(T) F   1. When people get along and help each other get the work done, everyone profits.

T   (F)   2. When working as part of a team, a person helps other team members only after his or her own work is done.

(T) F   3. High productivity is the goal of most work groups.

(T) F   4. Teams are more productive when each individual works to full capacity and helps other team members.

T   (F)   5. Highly productive employees are not expected to help their coworkers.

(T) F   6. A good team player solves problems with coworkers.

(T) F   7. Interactions among workers affect group productivity.

(T) F   8. Cooperation among workers is necessary for high group productivity.

T   (F)   9. Sharing information is *not* a good way to get ahead at work.

(T) F   10. Even those who work alone need to be team players to achieve work success.

Check Your Understanding

1. Why is cooperation an important human relations skill?
   <u>Sample response: Cooperation enables groups to be more productive. When people</u>
   <u>cooperate, they can accomplish more.</u>

2. Describe a team that you have worked on or observed, for example, school council or a sports team. Give an example of cooperation on this team.
   <u>Sample response: After the party in the gym was over, the clean-up team cooperated to take</u>
   <u>down all the decorations and dispose of the trash.</u>

3. How does teamwork help increase productivity?
   <u>When team members cooperate, they can work faster and more efficiently. As a result, they are</u>
   <u>more productive.</u>

4. Describe a team player.
   <u>A team player is a member of a team who cooperates and helps others get their work done.</u>

Coworker Relationships

DISCOVER

- what a good work relationship is.
- how relationships at work affect your happiness and success.
- how relationships affect each other.

Case: The Resentful Coworker

Aiesha, Kevin, and Jackie work in the public relations department of a large metropolitan hospital. Their department is small, so they work closely together. They work well as a team.

Aiesha is the creative force. She is the senior member of the department. She develops new promotions and arranges the educational programs. Kevin and Jackie like her and look to her when they have problems.

Kevin has been with the hospital a little more than a year. He was hired to handle media relations. He writes press releases, makes public statements, and creates the employee newsletter. Jackie is the newest member of the

Good communication can improve coworker relationships.

team. She was hired to work with both Kevin and Aiesha.

A few months after Jackie's arrival, Will, the department manager, noticed that she is a stronger writer than Kevin. Kevin's writing has been worrying Will. Now he has found a solution. Kevin is an excellent spokesperson for the hospital. He has also made good media contacts and gotten coverage of the hospital in both local and national news. Will decides to have Kevin focus on public speaking and media coverage. These key tasks are increasing and will need more of Kevin's time.

Will assigns Jackie to do the writing that Kevin had been doing. Kevin is not pleased. He feels he is a good writer. He resents having his responsibilities changed. He does his best to hide his feelings. Aiesha is aware of Kevin's anger. She tries to boost his ego by complimenting his work.

Kevin begins to avoid Jackie. She is aware that Kevin is unhappy, but it annoys her that he is taking it out on her. She needs information from Kevin to do her work. Jackie asks Aiesha

to get the information for her. Aiesha understands how both Jackie and Kevin feel. She is caught in the middle.

Now everyone in the office is unhappy. Aiesha offers support to Jackie and Kevin. She does all she can to avoid siding with one or the other.

Jackie decides the tension must stop and makes the first move. She invites Kevin to a meeting to get his views on stories for the next newsletter. During the meeting, she tells him how she feels. "I didn't make the decision to change your job," she says, "so I don't think it's fair that you're taking it out on me." Kevin is surprised to hear Jackie talk so openly about her feelings. He is also relieved to have the chance to clear the air.

Jackie knows that Kevin is proud of his people skills. She asks him to help her learn how to make contacts with the press. She also asks him for his ideas about the newsletter. She tells him that she is counting on him to show her the ropes. Kevin responds positively to Jackie's efforts to improve their relationship. He is relieved that the tension is gone.

DISCUSS

1. Describe Kevin's attitude toward his job.
   At first, Kevin seems dedicated to his job, but after his responsibilities are changed, he is resentful.

2. Does Kevin have a good reason for his attitude? Explain.
   Sample responses: Yes, his responsibilities were changed, and he feels that his skills are being criticized. No, he is being given more responsibilities in the areas in which he is strong.

3. What is your opinion of Kevin's behavior?
   Sample response: Kevin is acting immature by taking out his feelings on Jackie.

4. What would you have done in Jackie's situation?
   Sample response: I would have ignored the whole situation and just done my job.

ANALYZE

Relationships with **coworkers** influence your success and happiness at work. When relationships at work are good, you are likely to be happy and more productive. When you are productive and happy, your chance for career success increases. When relationships at work are bad, you are likely to be unhappy and less productive. When you are less productive and unhappy, your chance for career success decreases.

In your social life, you choose your relationships. In your working life, however, you have no choice. You have to work with the people on your team. You have to learn how to develop good work relationships.

What Is a Good Work Relationship?

You do not have to be best friends with your coworkers. It is not even necessary to like your coworkers. However, you do need to work positively with everyone at work. You need to get along with your coworkers so that company goals are reached. You need to interact with your coworkers in ways that do not cause tension, anger, or conflict.

A good work relationship has these characteristics:
- positive
- pleasant
- productive
- cooperative

People who work well together accomplish company goals. They also accomplish their own goals to be successful at work. They are able to talk openly about work and work-related issues with their coworkers. They can give and accept constructive criticism.

Types of Relationships at Work

People who work at the same job level as you do are called **peers**. In many companies, especially large ones, most of your interactions are with peers.

Workers also interact with people above them, such as supervisors, managers, and the owner or president of the company. Relationships with people above you are likely to be more formal. Workers may also interact with people below them.

The ranking of workers based on the level of their jobs is called a **hierarchy**. No matter where a person is in relation to you in the hierarchy, you must treat everyone with respect.

Good and Bad Relationships Can Create Problems

How you feel about each of your coworkers is influenced by your personal likes and dislikes. Your personality and your attitudes will fit better with some people than with others. How others feel about you is affected in the same way. However, keep in mind that the reason for good relationships at work is to achieve company goals. You will need to learn how to interact with everyone in a positive way.

Sometimes, friendships at work can be a problem. If you spend time talking about matters not related to work, you are not accomplishing work. You are wasting company time.

If you dislike someone, you are likely to create tension with that person. You may not even be aware of the tension you are causing. You may avoid each other, which may keep both of you from achieving work goals. Because Kevin avoided talking with Jackie, Jackie felt uncomfortable asking Kevin for information she needed to do her job.

Relationships Can Affect Others

Coworker relationships don't exist in a vacuum. If two people

become close friends, a third may feel excluded. If two people are angry with each other, the third may feel forced to take sides. Such situations distract all three people from getting work done.

Kevin's behavior was creating tension between him and Jackie. Their lack of communication threatened to interfere with the department's work. Aiesha was caught in the middle. She had a good relationship with each of them. She was feeling pressured to side with one or the other, but Aiesha knows that can create more problems. If she sided with one, she might have avoided the other. Such behavior could have lead Aiesha to become less productive.

She continues to be helpful and friendly to both. When one coworker comes to her to complain about the other, she refuses to listen and advises them to talk with each other. Aiesha is behaving in an **impartial** manner. Her behavior keeps the situation from getting worse. Aiesha's suggestion to talk with each other may be what led Jackie to take action.

Take Responsibility

You are responsible for the quality of your relationships. When you see a way to improve them, take action. Don't wait for the other person to make a move. Quite often, the other person is unable or unaware of what must be done.

Jackie may have felt that since Kevin was acting negatively toward her, Kevin should take the first step to improve the situation. However, Jackie was getting tired and stressed from the tension she felt. So *she* made the first move

by inviting Kevin to a meeting with her. When they were both feeling more comfortable with each other, she shared her frustrations with him. They were then able to discuss their relationship and the need to work together to make the company stronger.

Communication Is the Key to Good Relationships

Communication is the key to good relationships, both in and outside work. When there are relationship problems, communication often clears the air. However, you should never have a discussion when you or the other person is angry.

Sometimes, it is a good idea to let some time pass before taking action or talking with someone. Sometimes you or the other person needs time to calm down. Sometimes you need time to figure out what the real problem is, what is causing the behavior, and what the best solution is.

At times, it is better to let things slide and not take action. Avoiding action is most appropriate when you are being oversensitive. In other words, no one has done anything wrong, but you react as though they have. It is sometimes hard to determine when you are overreacting. To help see the situation more clearly, it is very helpful to talk with someone outside the situation, such as a trusted friend. Generally, however, you should discuss work-related problems with your supervisor.

DISCUSS

1. How did Aiesha create a good relationship between herself and both Jackie and Kevin?
   She did not take sides and supported each with positive comments.

2. Describe another outcome for this case, based on different behavior by Kevin.
   Sample response: Kevin might have been more mature about the change and taken the role of mentor to Jackie.

3. Describe another outcome, based on different behavior by Jackie.
   Sample response: Jackie might have gotten angry with Kevin, and the situation might have led to a shouting match.

4. Describe another outcome, based on different behavior by Aiesha.
   Sample response: Aiesha might have taken sides with Kevin and ruined her relationship with Jackie and her supervisor, Will.

APPLY

Case:
Working with Slackers

You are the most productive worker in your department. You enjoy your job and have good relationships with your coworkers. You sometimes find that you need to help them with their assignments. Lately, they need your help more and more. You wouldn't mind this so much if they were working hard. However, you are beginning to realize that they are slacking off because you have been bailing them out. You want to stop doing so much extra work.

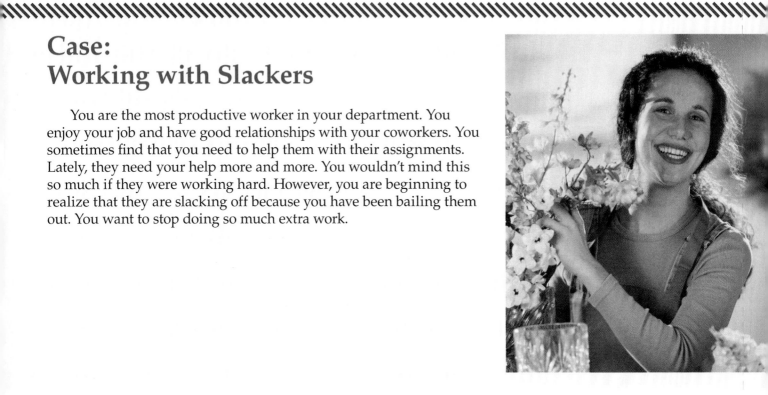

DISCUSS

1. List three options for dealing with your job situation.

   Option 1: **Sample response: You could refuse to continue doing their work and point out to your coworkers how poor their productivity is.**

   Option 2: **Sample response: You could complain to your supervisor.**

   Option 3: **Sample response: Gradually return responsibility to your coworkers for their own work. Volunteer your help less, but let them know that you are willing to show them how to do something or give advice.**

2. List the option you would choose, and explain why you would choose it.
   Sample response: Option 3 might be the best because it helps your coworkers get up to speed and start being more productive. Option 1 risks damaging your relationships with your coworkers. Option 2 risks damaging your relationship with your supervisor.

REVIEW

True or False

Circle *T* if the statement is true or *F* if the statement is false.

(T) F 1. Relationships with coworkers can influence your productivity.

T (F) 2. A person must like everyone at work.

(T) F 3. The result of good working relationships is achieving personal and company goals.

(T) F 4. It is okay if people do not like all their coworkers, as long as they have positive relationships.

(T) F 5. A person's attitudes affect relationships with his or her coworkers.

T (F) 6. Friendships at work never cause problems.

T (F) 7. Relationships at work have no effect on career success.

(T) F 8. Taking sides in an argument between two coworkers can damage a person's relationships with both.

(T) F 9. Communication is the most important element in developing good relationships.

(T) F 10. When someone is being oversensitive and has not been wronged, it is better *not* to take action.

Check Your Understanding

1. Describe a good work relationship.
   A good work relationship is positive, pleasant, productive, and cooperative.

2. Describe how relationships with peers can affect your happiness and success at work.
   If your relationships with peers are negative, you are likely to be unhappy and less successful at work.

3. When would it be better *not* to take action on a work relationship problem?
   If the other person has done nothing wrong and you are just overreacting, it is better to not take action.

Topic 5

Relationships with Supervisors

DISCOVER

- the nature of supervisor-employee relationships.
- how good coworker and supervisor relationships interact.
- the impact of supervisor-subordinate relationships on worker attitudes and productivity.

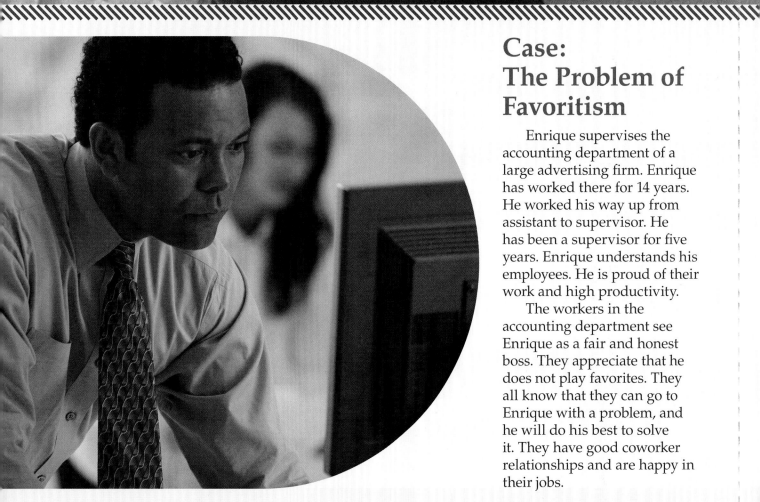

Case: The Problem of Favoritism

Enrique supervises the accounting department of a large advertising firm. Enrique has worked there for 14 years. He worked his way up from assistant to supervisor. He has been a supervisor for five years. Enrique understands his employees. He is proud of their work and high productivity.

The workers in the accounting department see Enrique as a fair and honest boss. They appreciate that he does not play favorites. They all know that they can go to Enrique with a problem, and he will do his best to solve it. They have good coworker relationships and are happy in their jobs.

Relationships with supervisors affect your work success and coworker relationships.

Recently, a new employee was hired. Jay is fresh out of school and eager to make good. Jay knows he has the skills to succeed in the company. He likes his coworkers, and they like him. Jay makes a good impression. He is quick to ask questions and thankful for advice from more experienced workers. They can see he will definitely be an asset to the department.

Jay and Enrique also hit it off. Enrique is reminded of himself 15 years ago. One evening, after working late on a project, Enrique and Jay stop to get a bite to eat. They discover how much they have in common. They both play basketball after work. They like the same kinds of movies. Jay even grew up in Enrique's old neighborhood. Jay asks Enrique's advice about his career. Enrique is pleased to be in a position to help a young man with so much on the ball.

Enrique and Jay get together occasionally to play or attend sports. Without being aware of it, Enrique starts giving Jay a little extra attention on the job. Jay's coworkers notice the growing friendship between Jay and their boss. When a new software system is considered, Enrique asks Jay to head the project. He has valid reasons for doing so. Jay recently took courses on just this type of system. However, Jay's coworkers see it differently. They are sure that Enrique has assigned the job to Jay because of their growing friendship.

The employees' jealousy begins to affect their relationships with Jay. They begin to see him as a threat to their careers. They are short with him when he comes to them for advice. They stop asking him to lunch with them. Jay feels excluded and cannot figure out why. He has no idea what he has done to upset his coworkers.

Their anger interferes with their previously excellent relationship with Enrique. They no longer see him as fair and impartial. They feel that he is favoring Jay. They begin putting less energy into their work. Productivity in the accounting department declines.

Enrique hears the grumblings. He observes that the others are avoiding Jay. He also is displeased with the decline in productivity. He had thought everything was going along so well. What is wrong?

DISCUSS

1. What do you think is wrong?
Sample responses: The workers are angry with the boss. Jay's coworkers are jealous of him.

2. How would you describe the relationship between Enrique and his staff before Jay was hired?
Sample response: Good. The employees thought Enrique was fair and honest.

3. How would you describe the relationship between Enrique and his staff after Enrique and Jay started socializing after work?
Sample response: Tense, angry. The employees thought Enrique was favoring Jay.

4. What is your opinion of the reaction of Jay's coworkers after Jay was assigned the software project?
Sample response: Jay's coworkers responded in a jealous and juvenile way.

ANALYZE

Your relationship with your supervisor can have a big impact on your success and happiness at work. Your **supervisor** is the person who assigns work to you, evaluates your work, and decides whether you get a raise. Your supervisor may also decide whether you get training opportunities. Relationships with supervisors and with coworkers have much in common. Both depend on effective communication between two people. However, there are some important differences.

Supervisors Set the Tone

Supervisors are responsible for setting the tone of the relationship with their subordinates. **Subordinates** are the workers they supervise. Some supervisors behave almost like coworkers. They socialize with their employees and treat them almost as peers. Others are all business.

Some supervisors are very good managers. Others are promoted to management jobs with little talent for the role. Some businesses provide training for new managers. However, many managers have no training in working with employees.

No matter what your supervisor is like, you must do your share to have a good relationship. Like all relationships between two people, it is a two-way street.

Business Environments Vary

Some businesses are casual. At those businesses, managers are flexible about time, dress, and behavior. There may be few rules, as long as everyone gets their work done. Other businesses are more formal. These businesses may have a dress code and strict rules about behavior. The tone of your workplace may depend on

the type of business conducted. For example, a bank usually has a formal atmosphere. A Web-site-development business might be more casual.

The personality of the department manager will also be a factor. You need to recognize what type of supervisor you have. What tone does he or she set? The way other employees interact is one important clue. Verbal and nonverbal communication will also give you clues.

The status of employees also needs to be considered. In some businesses, high-level staff members are friendly with each other but more formal with subordinates. When you enter a new workplace, noticing these things will help you adjust your behavior. Being able to adjust to fit in is a good human relations skill to have.

Supervisors Should Be Fair

In the case, you saw how a relationship with a supervisor could be almost too friendly. Jay's friendship with Enrique ruined his good relationship with his coworkers. It's natural for employees to have different relationships with the boss. Supervisors like some people more than they like others. However, the supervisor should treat everyone equally. A supervisor-subordinate friendship that creates jealousy is a problem.

Relationships with supervisors affect how coworkers feel about each other. Supervisors and employees need to be aware of how workplace friendships can affect others. An overly strong friendship with a boss can weaken coworker relationships. It can also cause **jealousy** among coworkers.

A manager must also avoid **favoritism**. Enrique's staff saw Enrique giving extra attention to Jay. The staff saw them socializing outside work. Jay then got the plum project. Enrique's behavior looked like favoritism. To some extent, it does not matter whether it really was or not. The appearance of favoritism is almost as bad as actual favoritism.

Enrique needs to work on his relationships with the other workers. He needs to act in a way that does not favor Jay. He should help all staff members understand their jobs and do them well. He should be a mentor to each subordinate. A **mentor** is someone who makes an effort to help you learn and succeed on the job.

Jay needs to spend time on his relationships with his coworkers. He needs to let them know that he is a hard-working member of the team. He will have to prove that he is getting ahead on **merit**—the actual quality of his work—and not because of his friendship with Enrique. Jay is finding out the potential problems with a mentor relationship with a supervisor.

As you work on having good supervisor-employee relationships, do not neglect your coworker relationships. Your success in your career and the productivity of your department depend on both relationships being good.

DISCUSS

1. How did the change in attitude of the staff affect productivity?
   The change to a negative attitude lowered productivity.

2. Do you think Enrique made any mistakes in his relationship with Jay? Explain.
   Enrique's socializing with Jay looked like favoritism. He should have socialized less with Jay and made more of an effort to work with the other members of the staff.

3. What can Enrique do to improve his relationship with his staff?
   He can spend more time with them, coaching them to do a better job.

4. What can Jay do to improve his relationships with his coworkers?
   He can pay more attention to his relationships with his coworkers. He can show them that he is a hard worker and is getting ahead on merit.

APPLY

Case:
New Job, New Supervisor

On your previous job, everyone was on a first-name basis. Your supervisor was less of a boss and more of a coworker and friend. When problems arose, everyone solved them together. Your supervisor never pulled rank. You could talk to her any time of the day; her office door was never closed.

You are having trouble adjusting to your new job. The working conditions are good, and your coworkers are pleasant. The supervisor, however, is very formal. He talks to you only about work and pays little attention to you otherwise. He is seldom available. Problems or questions are handled at a weekly staff meeting. At these meetings, the supervisor does most of the talking. You feel as if your ideas are not considered. He never asks how you are doing. You are wondering if you can ever make progress or be content working for a supervisor like him.

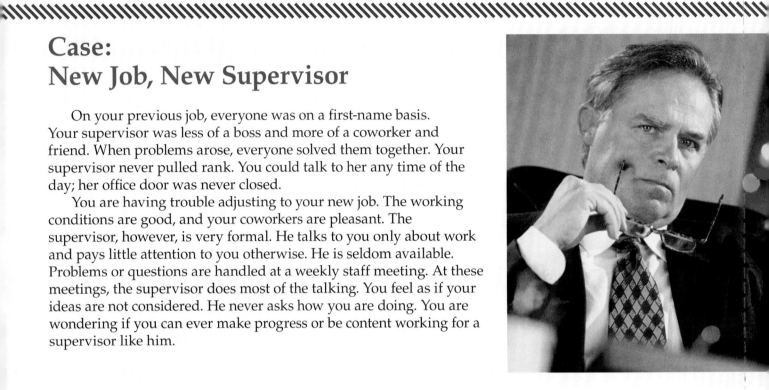

DISCUSS

1. List three options for working successfully with the new supervisor.

   Option 1: **Sample response: Have a meeting with the supervisor and tell him what he is doing wrong.**

   Option 2: **Sample response: Talk with a trusted coworker and ask for tips for getting along with the supervisor.**

   Option 3: **Sample response: Accept the supervisor, follow his rules, and work to improve your relationship with him.**

2. List the option you would choose, and explain why you would choose it.

   Sample response: Option 3. The new supervisor is not doing anything wrong. He just has a different style. If you change jobs, there is no assurance that your new boss would be any different. Your job is to follow the boss's lead and prove that you are a valuable employee. He may then value your judgment and suggestions.

REVIEW

True or False

Circle *T* if the statement is true or *F* is the statement is false.

(T) F 1. Good relationships with supervisors are essential to progress on the job.

T (F) 2. All businesses give managers formal training.

(T) F 3. Businesses have different standards for dress and behavior.

(T) F 4. The supervisor sets the tone for the relationship with subordinates.

T (F) 5. Effective communication is less important in relationships with supervisors than with coworkers.

(T) F 6. Verbal and nonverbal communication will give clues about the tone of the office environment.

(T) F 7. An overly friendly relationship with a boss can create problems with coworkers.

(T) F 8. A mentor helps less experienced workers make progress on the job.

(T) F 9. Judging an employee "on merit" means judging on how well he or she does the job.

T (F) 10. How workers relate to supervisors is much more important than how they relate to their coworkers.

Check Your Understanding

1. Describe a good supervisor-worker relationship from a coworker's viewpoint.
   The supervisor treats everyone equally and fairly. Assignments and rewards are based on merit, not favoritism.

2. How is a supervisor-worker relationship different from a coworker-coworker relationship?
   The supervisor should set the tone. The supervisor should be fair to all subordinates.

3. Imagine that you are having a problem with your supervisor. What could you do to improve it?
   Sample response: First, speak with your supervisor to determine what the problem is. Then brainstorm with your supervisor on ways to solve that problem.

4. How does favoritism by a supervisor create problems in a work group?
   The other members of the work group get jealous and may respond by putting less effort into their work.

5. How can a good relationship with your supervisor help you at work and in your career?
   A good relationship with your supervisor will ensure that you learn everything you need to know for your job. You will also perform better at work because you will be getting the feedback you need. You also may get more training and/or advancement opportunities.

Part 2
Attitudes at Work

Topic 6

Destructive Attitudes

DISCOVER

- the nature of destructive attitudes.
- the negative effect of destructive attitudes on the job.
- types of destructive attitudes.

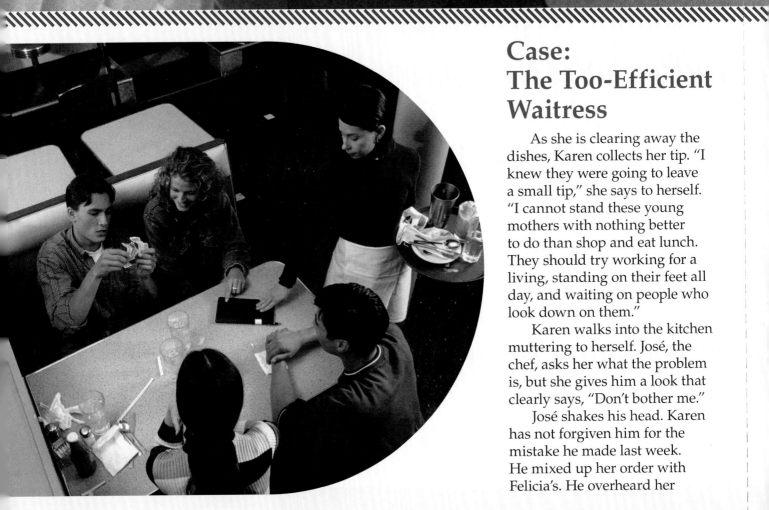

Case: The Too-Efficient Waitress

As she is clearing away the dishes, Karen collects her tip. "I knew they were going to leave a small tip," she says to herself. "I cannot stand these young mothers with nothing better to do than shop and eat lunch. They should try working for a living, standing on their feet all day, and waiting on people who look down on them."

Karen walks into the kitchen muttering to herself. José, the chef, asks her what the problem is, but she gives him a look that clearly says, "Don't bother me."

José shakes his head. Karen has not forgiven him for the mistake he made last week. He mixed up her order with Felicia's. He overheard her

The most productive worker in the world will not find career success with a bad attitude.

telling Felicia, "That José doesn't even try to improve his English. I can't stand these people who come here and think they don't have to learn our language." It still upsets him to think about it. He was glad Felicia defended him by telling Karen that it was an easy mistake to make.

The lunchtime crowd is slow today. Lately, business has been dropping off because of the new food court in the mall. As Karen waits on her tables, she can hear Felicia laughing with a group at a table across the room. "Honestly," Karen grumbles, "you'd think she was here to have fun instead of work."

Karen just wants to get people in and out as quickly as possible. She believes this is the sign of an efficient waitress. Most of the time, she does not worry about whether the customers like her. "Oh, sure," she thinks, "it's worth giving a little extra personal service to the businessmen. They have the money to tip well."

"Why does Felicia waste her time talking with those bums?" Karen wonders. "They're not going to leave a big tip. And those senior citizens! If they're too broke to tip, they should just stay home. Most of them can't read the menu, so you have to keep repeating it to them. Good thing they don't sit in my station anymore," Karen decides.

At the end of the shift, Dimitra, the restaurant manager, calls Karen into her office. As soon as the door closes, Karen begins complaining. "When Felicia lets customers linger over their coffee, I end up with more people at my station. It's not fair, and…" "That's enough, Karen." Dimitra stops her in mid-sentence. " As you know, our business is off. I have to let one waitress go. I'm afraid it's you."

"What are you talking about?" Karen is stunned. "I'm the fastest waitress you have! I never make mistakes. I get people in and out quickly. Felicia is not as good as I am."

Dimitra nods. "You are efficient, but your attitude upsets my customers. Felicia knows how to treat people so they want to come back. You, on the other hand, let your negative attitude affect your service. You almost chase people away. That's why I'm letting you go."

DISCUSS

1. What is your reaction to this case?
Sample responses: I don't understand why Karen was fired; she was so efficient. That Karen was so mean; I wonder why she wasn't fired sooner.

2. How would you describe Karen's attitude toward her job? toward her customers?
Sample responses: Karen wants to do a good job, but focuses only on efficiency. Karen does not like her customers; she may be jealous of them.

3. How did Karen's attitude affect her job performance?
Karen's negative attitude with customers was hurting the business.

4. Do you agree with Dimitra's decision? Explain.
**Sample responses: Yes, Karen's attitude was causing customers to go somewhere else.
No, the manager should have worked with Karen and given her another chance because she is so efficient.**

ANALYZE

The most productive worker in the world will not find career success with a bad attitude. No matter how you feel about others, do *not* let it show in the workplace. You might have to smile when you don't feel like it. You might have to swallow your pride or your anger. In the world of work, bad attitudes are destructive; and the thing that will be destroyed is your chance for success.

Combine Productivity with Positive Attitude

Karen was an efficient server. However, her negative attitude was destructive. It caused problems in her relationship with José. It caused customers to *not* return. Felicia was less efficient than Karen, but her constructive attitude encouraged customers to return. Dimitra could see this, and Felicia is the one who kept her job.

Today, most jobs are in the service industry. The **service industry** consists of jobs that provide a service, such as serving food, cutting hair, fixing a car, or providing medical care. A major part of a service job is interaction with customers. Whether you interact face-to-face, on the phone, or in writing, a constructive attitude is key. For success, your customer interactions must be positive. The service industry needs people who combine high productivity with a pleasant, positive attitude like Felicia's.

Prejudice and Discrimination

Karen might be surprised to be labeled a bigot, but her attitude indicates that she is. A **bigot** is a person who lacks tolerance for others who are different in some way. This lack of tolerance is usually based on negative beliefs about groups of people. Karen's negative attitude toward José was based on negative beliefs about immigrants.

Prejudice is hostility toward a group of people. Prejudice is usually based on external characteristics, such as race, gender, or age. A set of beliefs, often based on generalizations that are false, are then developed for that group of people. **Racism** is prejudice based on race, skin color, or ethnic heritage. **Ageism** is prejudice based on age. **Sexism** is prejudice based on gender.

Prejudice is an obstacle to good human relations because it prevents people from seeing each person as an individual. Prejudice cuts off communication between people.

Karen's racism has prevented her from seeing José as a productive member of the team.

Unlike Felicia, she does not see him as an individual, but as one of "those people." Not only has her attitude interfered with her developing a friendly relationship with José, but it has also interfered with her ability to work with him.

Karen's ageism prevents her from seeing senior citizens as individuals deserving of her attention. Instead, she looks at her elderly customers as part of a bothersome group.

Sexism negatively influences relationships among male and female employees, supervisors, and customers. An example of sexism is wrongly assuming a person cannot do a job simply because of his or her gender.

Prejudice can be responsible for destructive actions like impatience or abruptness. It can lead to arrogance or outright rudeness in your dealings with others. You may underestimate or overestimate the abilities of those you work with because of your attitude about their gender, race, ethnicity, or age.

Discrimination is the term for negative actions targeted at individuals based on their race, nationality, religion, or gender.

Laws protect employees from discrimination in the workplace. These same laws protect customers from discrimination by employees. As an employee, you represent the business, not yourself. Therefore, you are responsible for treating all customers with equal respect and courtesy. Treating everyone with respect is easy to do when you have a positive attitude and practice good human relations.

Oversensitivity

Oversensitivity is another destructive attitude that can limit your effectiveness. An oversensitive person takes slights and mistakes personally. Small incidents may become major upsets. The overly sensitive worker may spend too much time nursing wounded feelings. Meanwhile, work goes undone.

Selfishness

Selfish people have the attitude that their needs and concerns are more important than anyone else's. They are unable to put aside their own needs for the good of someone else. **Selfishness** may lead a worker to arrive late or leave early, never giving a thought to the effect on their coworkers who have to cover for them. Because they are primarily concerned with themselves, they are often tactless and inconsiderate in their dealings with others.

Dissatisfaction

Dissatisfaction is a destructive attitude that can take the joy out of a job for you and those who work with you. Nothing is right or good for the dissatisfied worker.

The boss is a jerk, the hours are bad, the raise was too small, and the customers are rude. One dissatisfied worker can spread negativity like a disease and reduce everyone's productivity.

For some people, always looking for the negative becomes a full-time occupation. Beware of dissatisfied coworkers. Don't let them change your positive attitude to a negative one. The energy you spend dwelling on the negatives can be put to better use. For example, if you find yourself in a job you really hate, look for another one. That's a much better use of your energy than complaining and being negative. In addition, if you do not show your dissatisfaction, you are more likely to get a good reference when you leave.

Counteract Destructive Attitudes

Destructive attitudes affect everything you do. They have a negative effect on your relationships with supervisors, coworkers, and customers. One way to avoid negative attitudes is to become aware of them.

To counteract destructive attitudes, study your responses to others. Because attitudes are often unconscious, you may not be aware of your destructive responses. To help you analyze your reactions, ask yourself the following questions:

- Do I have negative attitudes about a group of people?
- How do I respond to someone who is different from me?
- Do I get angry or rude to people for no obvious reason?
- Am I oversensitive about certain matters?
- Am I dissatisfied or negative about anything?

DISCUSS

1. How were Karen's attitudes destructive?
Karen has a negative attitude toward many types of people, which caused her to be rude to them. As a result, many customers did not want to return to the restaurant.

2. How were Felicia's attitudes constructive?
Felicia's positive and constructive attitude made people feel welcome and want to return to the restaurant.

3. How could Karen have been a better employee?
Sample response: Karen might have noticed that she had fewer customers and talked with Felicia about it. She might have tried to incorporate Felicia's attitudes and constructive behavior.

4. Now that Karen does not have a job, what advice would you give to her before she starts looking for a new job?
Sample response: Karen should think about the comments that the manager made about her effect on customers, and decide whether waitressing is the right job for her.

APPLY

Case:
You and the Malcontents

The shoe store you work for is often short-staffed. Many customers complain when the checkout lines are long. Customers often become angry when it takes you a long time to find the shoes they want.

You are unhappy because the customers are angry and rude. You try not to lose patience; but when someone yells at you, you speak up. You explain that you are doing the best you can. Sometimes customers leave before you return with their shoes, so you tell customers that it will take a while to get their size or color. You often add that if they don't want to wait, they can just say so and not waste your time.

Some customers have complained to your supervisor. She hints that you might lose your job if more complaints are received. You find it hard to understand why your future depends on the opinions of people who are obviously malcontents.

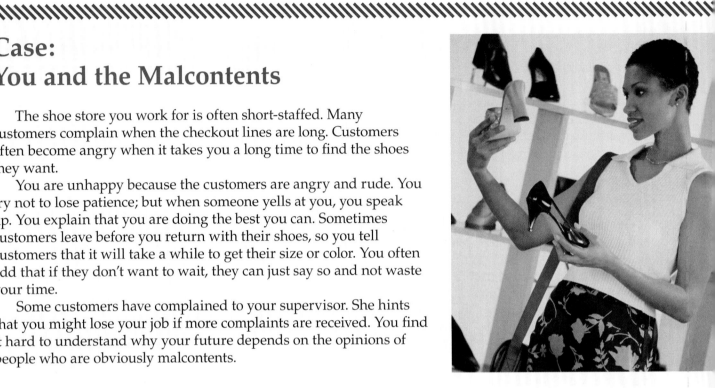

DISCUSS

1. List three options for dealing with your work situation.
   Option 1: **Sample response: Ignore the situation and trust that it will get better.**

   Option 2: **Sample response: Tell your supervisor that the complaining customers are not being fair to you.**

   Option 3: **Sample response: Meet with your supervisor and explain why you are having trouble serving all the customers. Ask for her help in figuring out how to do a better job.**

2. List the option you would choose, and explain why you would choose it.
   Sample response: Option 3. It provides the best chance of solving the problem and doing a better job.

REVIEW

True or False

Circle *T* if the statement is true or *F* if the statement is false.

T (F) 1. When workers are productive, they can get away with negative attitudes.

(T) F 2. Racism is a form of prejudice that is based on skin color or ethnic heritage.

T (F) 3. Racism, ageism, and sexism are three examples of constructive attitudes.

T (F) 4. Prejudices are based on true generalizations about groups of people.

(T) F 5. Destructive attitudes cut off communication between people.

T (F) 6. Oversensitivity means being very sensitive to the needs of others.

(T) F 7. Selfish workers are often tactless and inconsiderate in their relationships.

(T) F 8. One dissatisfied worker can reduce group productivity.

T (F) 9. A person *cannot* do anything to change a destructive attitude.

T (F) 10. People are usually aware of their negative attitudes and the destructive consequences that could result.

Check Your Understanding

1. What is a destructive attitude?
   <u>A destructive attitude is a negative attitude that causes people to act in destructive ways, such as being impatient or rude. Destructive attitudes can also lead to discrimination.</u>

2. Why do jobs in the service industry require constructive attitudes?
   <u>Workers in the service industry constantly interact with others. Their main product is service, so their attitudes must be positive and constructive to have a positive effect on their customers.</u>

3. Give an example of how a destructive attitude can cause problems on the job.
   <u>Sample response: The waitress with the destructive attitude caused customers to never return; she also hurt the feelings of coworkers.</u>

4. Name six types of destructive attitudes.
   <u>Racism, ageism, sexism, oversensitivity, selfishness, dissatisfaction</u>

5. Describe a destructive attitude. What can you do to counteract it?
   <u>Sample response: Ageism is being rude to older people just because they are older. To counteract this attitude, get to know people who are older than you are by volunteering at a senior center.</u>

Constructive Attitudes

DISCOVER

- what a constructive attitude is.
- the difference between a positive attitude and a constructive attitude.

Case: Employee of the Month

Jada and Tia are salespeople in the sportswear department of a local clothing store. They are both good workers and enjoy their jobs. They stay informed about fashion trends and attend fashion workshops offered by the various manufacturers.

The store is finding it hard to compete with the large chains that are moving into the area. The owner, Mariko, believes that one way to increase sales is to reward the store's best salespeople. She announces an award for employee of the month. The winner will receive a $100 bonus. His or her picture will be displayed for the month. The employees like the idea.

A constructive attitude is more than just a smile.

DISCUSS

1. Describe Jada's attitude.
   Sample response: Jada reaches out to her customers; she does not wait for them to ask for help. Jada actively helps her customers and takes extra steps to close the sale.

2. Describe Tia's attitude.
   Sample response: Tia is very friendly, but she does not reach out to the customers; she waits for them to come to her.

3. What is the difference between Jada's and Tia's attitudes?
   Sample response: Jada is more helpful to her customers.

4. Who would you have chosen for employee of the month? Why?
   Sample responses: Jada, because she reaches out to her customers and her customers ask for her. Tia, because she was nice and she didn't bother the customers if they did not want to be bothered.

The store has many good employees. Since sales have been rising in the sportswear department, Mariko has narrowed her choice to Jada or Tia. To make her choice, she spends some time watching them at work. The first thing she notices is that Jada seems to know her customers. Most of the regulars go straight to her for help. In fact, when business is slow, there might be two or three regular customers waiting for Jada, while Tia is not busy.

It doesn't take Mariko long to figure out why this happens. She sees that Tia is efficient and friendly. Tia smiles at customers, but waits for them to ask for help. She doesn't offer suggestions or point out sales. She leaves customers alone to search for colors or sizes. Meanwhile, Jada offers suggestions for putting outfits together. She helps customers find sale items and offers to place special orders. Mariko sees why sales are rising. Jada takes the extra steps to close the sale.

Mariko knows who her first employee of the month will be: Jada. Jada provides the extra service that closes sales and brings customers back. Mariko also decides that she will ask Jada to offer a workshop on sales techniques to all the salespeople. In this way, Mariko will help all her salespeople improve their skills and make more sales.

ANALYZE

A positive attitude alone cannot make up for a lack of human relations skills. A nice smile cannot take the place of putting extra effort into helping a customer. Jada and Tia are equally positive and friendly workers. Jada stood out because her constructive attitude made her the more valuable employee.

A **constructive attitude** is more than just a smile. A friendly face is a good start, but a constructive attitude is more than that. A constructive attitude combines friendliness with taking action to get positive results.

This approach leads to greater productivity. In today's service industries, a constructive attitude is highly valued.

Action Is Key

The key to a constructive attitude is action. People who have constructive attitudes go out of their way to do something that gets positive results. A salesperson searches for the right style and color for a customer. A restaurant server prepares a special request. An engineer discovers that a weld is weak and fixes it before it breaks.

People who have constructive attitudes are **proactive**. They do not wait to be asked to do something. They use their minds and creativity to figure out what to do before being asked or before a problem occurs.

Proactive workers are more productive. They do not waste time because they do not wait to be asked. If they finish a task early, they find additional tasks or ask their supervisors for more work.

A Constructive Attitude Creates Goodwill

People with constructive attitudes create goodwill. **Goodwill** is a positive feeling that occurs when someone

does something nice for you. A business wants its customers to feel goodwill toward the business. One way to build goodwill is to have salespeople who actively help the customers.

It is one thing to say, "I'm here to help you." It is another thing to act in a helpful way. If you say you are there to help, but make little effort, people will not be impressed. If you take the time to learn what customers want or bring them samples to try, they will remember you. Even if they do not find what they want that day, they are likely to return to your store for your personal service.

Jada created goodwill toward the store by her actions. Jada made her customers feel special and valued because she took action to help them. These good feelings encourage customers to return. In this way, workers with constructive attitudes help their companies succeed.

A Constructive Attitude Helps You Succeed

Supervisors appreciate workers with a constructive attitude. Such workers usually are more productive and more successful with customers. Supervisors do not have to worry about proactive workers. Proactive workers will come to the supervisor when they run out of work or have a question.

A constructive attitude also helps you when you have a bad day. Personal problems can interfere with your focus at work. It's hard to smile at a customer or coworker when you are worried about something. A constructive attitude helps you focus on your job. It helps you be active and involved while working. Being actively involved in your work helps you put aside your problems and do a better job while at work.

DISCUSS

1. Which salesperson has a constructive attitude?
Jada
2. What does this salesperson do to communicate her constructive attitude to customers?
Jada offers suggestions, points out sales, helps customers search for colors and sizes, puts outfits together, offers to place special orders.
3. Do you agree that the right person was chosen as Employee of the Month? Explain.
Sample response: Yes, Jada has a constructive attitude and goes out of her way to help customers. As a result, her customers like her, come back to the store, and ask for her.

APPLY

Case:
Handling a Bad Day

You have had a terrible morning. The shower splashed all over the bathroom floor. You spilled breakfast cereal on your favorite shirt and had to change clothes. You were late for school and you had an argument with a friend over your weekend plans. As you dash to your part-time tutoring job after school, your mother calls to tell you that your favorite uncle was rushed to the hospital with chest pains. As you arrive late at the tutoring center, a coworker cheerily asks how you are. She wants to know if you can work with her student today because she has to leave early.

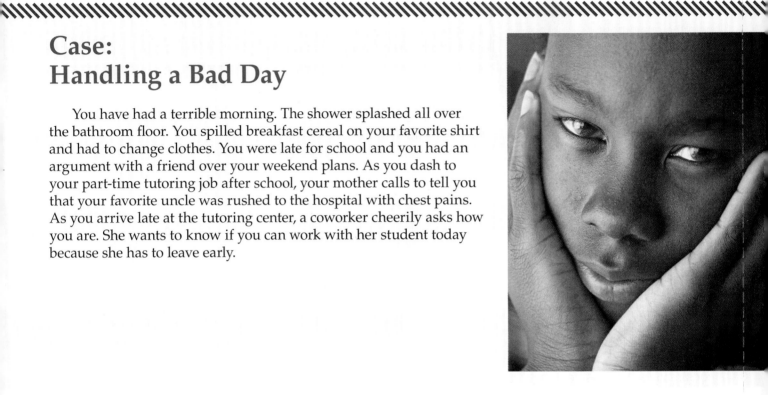

DISCUSS

1. List four options for responding to your coworker.
   Option 1: __Sample response: Say "no" in a sharp voice and stomp away.__

   Option 2: __Sample response: Tell your supervisor what happened and ask to be excused for the evening.__

   Option 3: __Sample response: Put your personal problems in the background and act upbeat.__

   Option 4: __Sample response: Say, "I've had a rough day, but, sure, I can work with your student."__

2. List the option you would choose, and explain why you would choose it.
   __Sample response: Option 4. By telling your coworker briefly about your day, she will be able to understand why you are not as cheerful as you usually are. By being brief, you do not waste time talking and get right to work.__

REVIEW

True or False

Circle *T* if the statement is true or *F* if the statement is false.

T (F) 1. A positive attitude is all that is needed to have good human relations.

(T) F 2. A constructive attitude is more than a friendly face and a smile.

T (F) 3. To create goodwill with a customer, the salesperson must solve the problem.

(T) F 4. Positive action is the key to a constructive attitude.

T (F) 5. Proactive workers waste a great deal of time.

T (F) 6. A smile on a person's face is always a sign of a constructive attitude.

T (F) 7. Discovering the interests and needs of others is important only in personal relationships.

(T) F 8. Workers with constructive attitudes tend to create goodwill in their customers.

(T) F 9. Customers tend to shop at stores that make them feel special.

(T) F 10. A constructive attitude can help workers cope with bad days.

Check Your Understanding

1. Explain the difference between a positive attitude and a constructive attitude.
   <u>A positive attitude includes friendliness, optimism, and cheerfulness, but not action. A</u>
   <u>constructive attitude includes the attributes of a positive attitude plus the behavior of taking</u>
   <u>action to solve problems.</u>

2. How can a constructive attitude help you succeed at work?
   <u>If you have a constructive attitude at work, you are more likely to focus on your job, waste less</u>
   <u>time, and take actions before problems arise.</u>

3. What advice would you give to Tia to help her have a constructive attitude?
   <u>Sample response: I would suggest that Tia first ask, "How can I help you?" Then she should</u>
   <u>escort the customers to where they can find what they are looking for.</u>

4. Describe goodwill.
   <u>Sample response: Goodwill is the positive way your customers will feel when you take action</u>
   <u>to solve their problems and make them feel special.</u>

Topic 8
Morale

DISCOVER

- what morale is.
- how high morale can lead to success at work.
- how low morale can lead to problems at work.

Case:
The Perfect Job

Caitlin is the receptionist for a busy nail salon. She enjoys working with the manager and her coworkers. She likes getting free nail services. However, Caitlin's goal is to work with animals.

One morning, Caitlin's dad notices an ad for a receptionist at the local pet hospital. He says to Caitlin, "This sounds like the perfect job for you." Caitlin agrees and goes to the hospital that afternoon to apply for the job.

The interview goes very well, and the office manager offers Caitlin the job on the spot. Caitlin accepts and resigns from her job at the nail salon.

Morale influences success at work.

DISCUSS

1. Describe Caitlin's attitude toward her job at the nail salon.
   Sample response: Positive; she enjoys her job.
2. Describe Caitlin's attitude toward her job at the pet hospital.
   Sample response: Negative; she feels frustrated, unappreciated, and overwhelmed.
3. How do you think Jovan and Jessica feel about their jobs?
   Sample response: It is hard to know for sure. They may love their jobs.
4. What would you have done in Caitlin's situation?
   Sample responses: I would have quit and gone back to my old job. I would have stuck it out just to be in an animal hospital.

On her first day at the pet hospital, Caitlin meets her coworker, Jovan. Jessica, the business manager, is her new boss. Caitlin takes her place at the reception desk. During her interview, Caitlin hadn't noticed how small and crowded the reception area was. Her desk is crammed into a tight corner and piled high with papers and files. Pet owners and their pets come and go all day long. The activity is nonstop.

Jessica tells Jovan to train Caitlin. Jovan was the receptionist before he went back to school to study veterinary technology. He now prepares instruments for surgery and helps handle the animals during examinations.

Caitlin is excited about learning her new job. She loves to bring order to chaos, and the desk looks as if no one has done any filing in months. Each veterinarian has his or her own appointment cards and books. However, Jovan is constantly interrupted as he tries to explain things to Caitlin. She tries hard to make sense of Jovan's incomplete instructions, but it is difficult.

Caitlin loves seeing the pets and meeting their owners. However, the office is very busy. All day, it's "sign this form, please" and "what method of payment, please." There is barely time to say hello or pet the animals. The veterinarians just nod and rush past her desk.

Because her training is so incomplete, she has many questions. She begins to see that the other workers are too busy to give her much help. Jessica is always too busy or out of the office on business.

As time goes by, Caitlin feels more and more unhappy at work. She spends most of her day on the phone or doing paperwork. There is little interaction with her coworkers or with the pet owners and pets. Caitlin does not feel appreciated or part of a team.

After two months, Caitlin learns that her former job at the nail salon is available. Caitlin resigns her job at the pet hospital and returns to the nail salon.

ANALYZE

Morale refers to feelings and attitudes about the workplace. Managers are concerned about the morale of individuals in their work groups. They are also concerned about the morale of the work group as a whole.

High Morale Can Lead to Business Success

When morale is high, workers are confident. They are cheerful, enthusiastic about work, and willing to perform assigned tasks. The group feels unified and dedicated to reaching goals. A workplace where morale is high is a pleasant place to work. Employees are positive, and their high morale shows in their interactions with customers. Workers perform better on their jobs, and customers are satisfied, too. High morale can lead to higher sales and business success.

Low Morale Can Lead to Poor Performance

When morale is low, the general attitude is negative. Workers dislike their work and are less willing to perform assigned tasks. The group does not care about goals or the future of the company. A workplace with low morale is an unpleasant place to work. Customers can tell if the morale of a business is low. The employees are likely to be rude and unhelpful toward customers. Low morale can lead to unhappy

customers who do not return to the business.

Low morale can negatively affect job performance. If you are unhappy with your job responsibilities or your work environment, you may start to care less about your work. Why work hard, if no one notices or appreciates you? If you receive only negative feedback from supervisors or coworkers, you may start to feel resentful. You may then dread going to work. A negative attitude may lead to being less careful about work, so performance may fall. Workers may be tempted to fake illness and skip work.

The Job Situation Affects Morale

Caitlin began her job at the pet hospital with high morale. She expected to like any job where she would be around animals. She assumed that her new coworkers would be like those on the job at the salon. Several factors led her morale to fall as time went on.

One of these factors was the workspace. Crowded and cramped, the space was small and poorly organized. Caitlin was used to working in more spacious surroundings. The lack of good training procedures was another factor. It was hard for Caitlin to know how to do her job when she lacked information.

Caitlin's coworkers were another factor in her low morale. They were too busy to chat with Caitlin. Caitlin interpreted their behavior as unfriendliness, and she no longer looked forward to going to work. The business manager and the doctors were also distant, adding to Caitlin's

feeling that she was not part of a team.

Your Confidence Affects Your Morale

How you feel about yourself influences your level of **confidence**. Confidence means you feel sure of yourself. Some people have a shaky sense of confidence. They may lose confidence when they start a new job. Some people are confident regardless of the situation.

If you fear that you are not up to the challenge of your job, you may lose confidence. If you lose confidence, it may cause your morale to drop. As you gain knowledge and experience, your confidence is likely to increase. Once you prove to yourself that you are capable of handling the new responsibilities, your morale is likely to rise again.

Find Out the Cause of Low Morale

Caitlin started with high morale, but was soon unhappy. It is common to experience changes in your level of morale at work. Sometimes this happens from day to day. Sometimes your morale changes over a long period of time. As your goals change, your satisfaction level with your job may change. Caitlin decided to leave the job she enjoyed at the nail salon because she wanted to pursue her goal of working with animals.

If you have long periods of low morale, you need to discover why. Ask yourself these questions:

- **Are you doing what you want to do?** Are you and the job a good fit? Caitlin enjoyed working with people. She liked to feel needed. One reason for her unhappiness and low morale at the pet hospital was that her contacts with patients were so limited. She missed being able to help her customers and coworkers as she did in the nail salon.

- **Are your expectations too high?** You may feel that you are not progressing fast enough. You may have expected to receive a promotion or raise that did not materialize. It might help to reevaluate your expectations and see if they are realistic. Caitlin expected to feel as comfortable at the pet hospital as she did at the salon. She assumed she would be welcomed and treated as a member of the team right away. Was this unrealistic?

- **Are you overqualified for your job?** Being **overqualified** means you have more knowledge and skills than a job requires. If your work is not challenging enough, your morale might fall. You might get very bored. You might feel disappointed in yourself. You might feel that you need a job with more challenge. For this very reason, few employers will hire someone who seems overqualified for a job.

Quitting Is a Last Resort

Quitting should *not* be your first answer to low morale. There are often many things you can do to improve the situation.

In Caitlin's situation, should she have given it more time? Could she have talked to her supervisor about her concerns?

How do you react when your expectations are not met? Speaking up and making constructive suggestions can improve things. Staying quiet and leaving a job is not always the answer.

If Caitlin had remained at the doctor's office, she might have helped improve the office morale. She could have shared with Jessica some ideas for making the office run more smoothly.

Discuss Low Morale with Your Supervisor

If you are struggling with low morale, talk to your supervisor. Describe your problem and see if he or she can offer any help. Do not focus on a laundry list of complaints or personal attacks on your coworkers. Keep the focus of the conversation on concrete problems that can be solved.

Before having the conversation, make a list of the concrete problems. For each problem, develop a solution. For example, Caitlin had trouble keeping up with the patients because the files were so disorganized. She might suggest a better filing system and request that she be given time just to organize the files. Make it clear that you want to make things work better for the group and for the business as a whole.

DISCUSS

1. Describe Caitlin's morale at the nail salon.
   Caitlin's morale was high. She was cheerful, enthusiastic, and productive.

2. Describe Caitlin's morale at the pet hospital.
   Caitlin's morale was low. She was unhappy, frustrated, and felt unappreciated.

3. How did Caitlin's morale change after a few days on the job at the pet hospital?
   Caitlin's morale went from high to low.

4. Instead of quitting, what could Caitlin have done to improve her situation at the pet hospital?
   Sample responses: She could have made an appointment to discuss her concerns with her boss. She could have asked for more training. She could have started taking vet technician courses in veterinary technology.

APPLY

Case:
An Insecure Job

Your company is in financial trouble. Several people have been laid off, and there are more layoffs coming. Your supervisor has told you that your job is secure; but with so many people being fired, it is hard to believe. Going to work is becoming more depressing every day. Coworkers have stopped working; instead, they are discussing the latest layoff or debating the company's future. You thought you would be able to advance your career at this company. Now you wonder what the future holds for your employer. In spite of the turmoil, you work hard at staying upbeat.

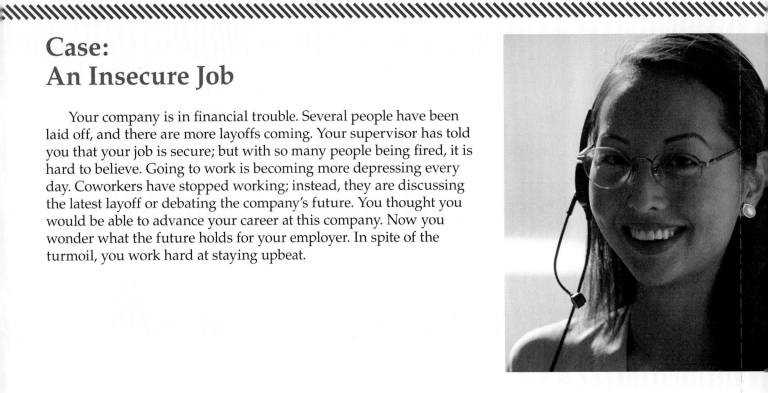

DISCUSS

1. List three options for dealing with your job situation.
   Option 1: **Sample response: Believe your supervisor and ignore your concerns and your coworkers' behavior.**

   Option 2: **Sample response: Look for a new job.**

   Option 3: **Sample response: Accept that you are going through a period of low morale and work through your worries.**

2. List the option you would choose, and explain why you would choose it.
   Sample response: Option 3. It is a bad idea to give up on a good job, and many workplaces go through tough times with change, uncertainty, and low morale. Meanwhile, you can still keep your eyes open for other opportunities. As long as you are with this employer, you should focus on your work and do the best job you can.

REVIEW

True or False

Circle *T* if the statement is true or *F* if the statement is false.

T (F) 1. Morale refers to how productive a person is at work.

(T) F 2. A workplace where morale is high is nearly always a pleasant place to work.

T (F) 3. High moral has no impact on business success.

T (F) 4. Generally, workers are unaware of worker morale at a business.

(T) F 5. Low morale can lead to poor performance.

T (F) 6. A person's morale is affected only by his or her own attitude and the attitude of the work group.

T (F) 7. A cramped workspace causes low morale.

(T) F 8. Lack of confidence can lead to low morale.

(T) F 9. Discussing problems with the supervisor is a good way to improve low morale.

T (F) 10. Quitting is the best solution for problems at work.

Check Your Understanding

1. Describe a person with high morale.
   <u>A person with high morale is confident about his or her ability to do the job and is cheerful,</u>
   <u>enthusiastic about work, and willing to perform assigned tasks.</u>

2. Describe a person with low morale.
   <u>A person with low morale is negative. He or she does not like the work and is less willing to</u>
   <u>perform assigned tasks.</u>

3. Explain how low morale in a work group can lower sales.
   <u>When people at work have low morale, they may be rude and less helpful to customers. As a</u>
   <u>result, customers will have a bad experience at the store and decide not to return. Then sales</u>
   <u>will fall.</u>

4. Describe two ways to handle low morale.
   <u>Sample response: Figure out the reasons why you have low morale. Talk with your supervisor</u>
   <u>about ways to solve the problems that are causing you to have low morale.</u>

Topic 9

Handling Stress on the Job

DISCOVER

- the relationship between stress and aggression.
- the role of attitude in lowering your level of stress.
- how to deal with stress.

Case: The Stressed-Out Manager

"I'm quitting," shouts Juan. "I can't take it any more!"

"Now wait a minute," his manager, Susan, responds. "All I asked was that you be more careful when you proofread. Several promotional letters went out with typos in them. Errors hurt sales."

"Those so-called errors could have been caused by the computer," Juan replies. "Did anyone think of that?"

"Well, Juan," says Susan, "no one wants to hear that. We can't rely on computers to find all our mistakes. When anything goes wrong, marketing jumps on me because I'm the head of word-processing."

Stress is a normal part of life.

DISCUSS

1. What triggered Juan's anger?
   Juan's boss asked him to be more careful.
2. What is your opinion of Susan as a boss?
   Sample responses: Susan is a good boss who tries to help her subordinates. Susan is too soft.
3. What would you have done if you had been Juan?
   Sample responses: I would have quit. I would not have said anything and tried harder to do my job.
4. What would you have done if you had been Susan?
   Sample responses: I would have fired Juan. I would have given him advice, the way Susan did.

"Yeah, and then you jump on us supervisors," Juan says. "All the heat comes down on us. I'm sick of it, and I'm quitting."

"Now, don't do anything hasty," Susan cautions. "You worked hard for your promotion to supervisor. You've been a supervisor for only a short time, and you have been doing well. Don't let one little criticism stop you. It is part of the job."

"Sure, it goes with the job," Juan agrees, "but I do a good job under tough conditions. We have to meet a quota for producing the letters. If I send too many back for correction, we don't make our goals. Then everyone gets mad at me. If I slip up once in a while and a small error gets through, then you and marketing get on my back. It's a no-win situation for me."

"You're paid well for what you do," Susan reminds him.

"I know I make a lot more than I did before the promotion, but then I didn't take the job home with me. Now it's on my mind all the time. I worried all last night about the letters I approved yesterday. I rechecked them this morning, and they are okay; but that didn't give me back the lost sleep."

"I appreciate your carefulness," Susan explains, "and you are one of my best supervisors. However, you have to learn how to handle stress. Quitting is not the answer. There is some stress on every job."

"How do you handle it?" Juan asks.

"First," Susan says, "I accept the fact that there will be some stress on the job. Then I make a schedule for the tasks I must accomplish. I keep track of each task and its due date. If I get off track, I analyze the situation to determine how to get back on track. If the problem is bigger than I can handle, I consult with my boss.

"In addition, I make sure to take care of my health so that I don't react to stress by bad habits. I eat healthy foods, exercise, and read before bedtime to help me sleep. When I'm away from work, I do not think about work. I make sure I have quality time with my family and friends. That way, I can concentrate fully on work when I am here."

Juan thinks over what Susan has said. "Thanks, Susan. What you said makes sense. I will try your suggestions."

ANALYZE

Stress is a feeling of tension that results when you have problems reaching a goal. When you are late for an appointment and get stuck in traffic, you feel stressed. When you can't find the term paper you spent hours writing, you feel stressed. There are ways to avoid stress—you can make a habit of leaving earlier for appointments and filing your papers more carefully. However, there is no way to avoid *all* stress. Stress is an inevitable part of life. In fact, some stress is actually good for you.

Stress Is Related to Destructive Attitudes

Stress at work may be the cause of a destructive attitude or it may be the result of it. Juan's attitude toward his job was destructive. His career was progressing well, but he was willing to give up his success to avoid stress. His stress was caused by taking on new responsibilities and having to meet high standards based on other people's work. His lack of a solution for his problem was the cause of his destructive attitude.

If you approach your job with destructive attitudes, you will limit your opportunity for growth. Every job has problems; thinking about quitting is not the solution to problems on the job. Juan made a wise choice by talking over his feelings with Susan, his supervisor. She gave him good advice that might help him turn things around. Developing constructive attitudes will help you find solutions and eliminate stress.

Find Ways to Handle Stress

Stress is a normal part of life. It does not just go away. You need to find ways to handle situations that cause you stress. If you do not handle your stress, it can build up. The build-up of stress can negatively affect your performance, your attitude, and even your health.

How you deal with stress on the job can affect your career positively or negatively. Even in a job you love, you will experience stress at some point. There are acceptable and unacceptable ways to deal with stress.

Unacceptable Ways to Relieve Stress

Stress can cause feelings of anger and frustration. It can be tempting to act out these feelings by **aggressive behavior**. Aggressive behavior is behavior that is hostile or destructive, such as yelling, throwing things, slamming doors, or hitting something or someone. Aggressive behavior will damage your career. When you react to stress with aggressive behavior, you are taking out your negative feelings on the people with whom you work. Aggressive behavior is unacceptable at work. It is often grounds for being fired immediately.

Verbal aggression can also cause problems at work. Verbal aggression is speaking in a hostile or angry way. Juan's verbal aggression was his threat to quit. Threatening to quit is an unacceptable way to deal with stress. Threats to quit might make you feel better; however, they serve no constructive purpose.

The cause of your stress is still there, and your poor performance will bring negative consequences sooner or later. Also, if you threaten to quit, your boss might just respond, "That's fine with me. Your resignation is accepted."

Juan let his stress build to the point where he couldn't sleep. Then, when his manager made a reasonable request, he reacted angrily. He has damaged his relationship with his supervisor. Susan understood Juan's anger and was sympathetic. However, now she may worry about his ability to handle increased responsibilities. Unless Juan is able to change, it is doubtful that he will get another promotion. In fact, Susan might decide to take away his management responsibilities.

Sometimes, you may find yourself on the receiving end of anger or aggression from supervisors, coworkers, or customers. Your supervisor may be stressed after reading the latest error report. If you are the next person to walk into the room, you may find that your boss reacts to stress by speaking to you angrily. Whenever someone speaks angrily to you, do not respond with anger. Angry arguments can damage relationships. Respond calmly to the person. In many cases, nothing that you do can calm angry people, and the best thing to do is to say that you will talk to them later.

Acceptable Ways to Relieve Stress

When you feel your stress level rising, try to release it in an acceptable way. It is a good idea to seek the advice of a person who is not involved in the situation. However, be wise about your choice. Venting stress to the wrong person can backfire. Avoid criticizing your boss, your coworkers, and your company. Words spoken in anger or to the wrong person can come back to haunt you.

Talk with Someone You Trust

Talking with someone you trust can give you insight into your situation. Sometimes just the act of talking is reassuring and relieves stress. It might be best to choose someone outside the workplace. If you know someone who has experience in the workplace, he or she may be able to give you suggestions on ways to handle your situation. A friend or family member might be able to help you see things more clearly. Make sure the person you confide in is someone with a positive attitude. The last thing you need is **negative reinforcement**. Negative reinforcement occurs when you talk with someone who encourages your negative attitudes.

Become Physically Active

Maintaining a constructive attitude when stressed will be easier if you have an outlet for your negative feelings. Physical activity is an excellent way to discharge stress. Walk, run, bicycle, swim, play handball, clean your room, vacuum, or cut the grass. At work, do something physical if you possibly can. Reorganize a messy storage room, scrub the office coffeepot, or use your break to take a brisk walk.

Write in Your Journal

If talking does not help, try writing about the situation in your journal. Putting your feelings in writing can help you to analyze them. Are your feelings justified, or are you being too sensitive? Are you blaming others or taking responsibility? You might also write about several ways to resolve the problem. Seeing the options in black and white may help you make a good choice for solving the problem.

It is generally not advisable to send written communication about a work problem. Angry spoken words may eventually be forgotten. Angry written words will be around long after the situation that prompted them is gone. Such communications will probably be placed in your permanent human resources file for all future supervisors to read.

If the situation is serious, such as a physical threat, you should go to your company's human resources department and seek help from the appropriate person.

Put Work in Its Place

Dealing with stress at work is easier if you have a balanced life. Family, friends, and outside interests can help you deal with stress. These outside activities will help you put work in perspective as one part of your life.

A balance between work and personal life is especially important as you advance in your career. Meeting goals, such as lowering costs, can consume a great deal of energy. If work is all you do and all you have, then the stress you encounter at work may become too much. Having close friends outside work will help you deal with job stress. Doing activities you like will help you approach your job with a positive attitude. Spending time away from work with people whose company you enjoy also relieves stress.

DISCUSS

1. What was causing Juan's stress?
   Sample responses: Stress at work. Criticism from his boss. The difficulty of the job.
2. Was Juan angry with Susan?
   Sample responses: Yes, because she criticized him. No, he was really angry with himself for making a mistake. No, he was angry because the job is hard.
3. List two other ways that Juan could have handled his stress.
   Sample response: He could have arranged a meeting with his boss to discuss the situation. He could have analyzed his anger and found other ways to manage it, such as exercising.

APPLY

Case:
The Delayed Promotion

You are transferred to a new department. You do not want to accept the transfer because you will have to work evening hours. You are assured that by accepting the transfer, you will make progress toward a supervisory position. You accept the transfer, and your manager is pleased with your work. After a year on the job, two of your coworkers in your previous department have been promoted. You feel that your move has not paid off. Your department budget has been cut back, and your workload has increased. You feel you deserve a promotion as promised. You tell your supervisor that you were led to believe you would be promoted when you took the transfer. She tells you to be patient; it will happen soon. The next month a coworker receives the promotion instead. You are furious.

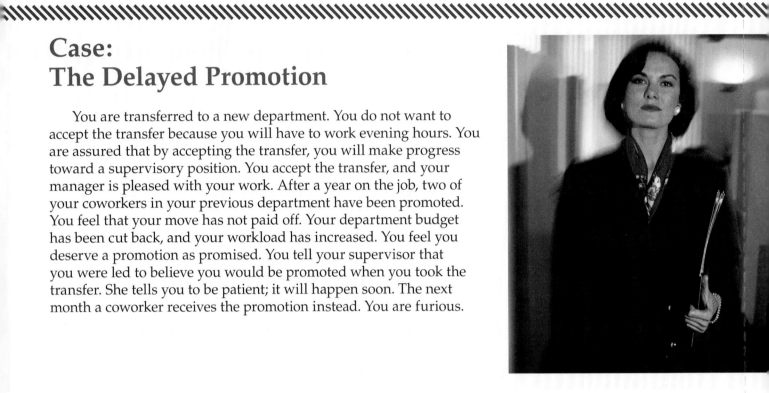

DISCUSS

1. List three options for dealing with your job situation.
   Option 1: __Sample response: March into the supervisor's office and tell her how unfair it is that you have not gotten the promotion you were promised.__

   Option 2: __Sample response: Complain to your coworkers about how unfair management is.__

   Option 3: __Sample response: Take a walk and calm down, then ask for a meeting with the supervisor to discuss why you were not promoted.__

2. List the option you would choose, and explain why you would choose it.
   __Sample response: Option 3. Getting angry either at the supervisor or with coworkers is not productive. If you find out why you were not promoted, then you can take steps to improve. If you find out that there is no promotion opportunity for you, you can then consider looking for a new job.__

REVIEW

True or False

Circle *T* if the statement is true or *F* if the statement is false.

(T) F 1. Every job involves some degree of stress.

(T) F 2. Stress can be the cause of a destructive attitude.

T (F) 3. Aggressive behavior is one acceptable way of dealing with stress.

T (F) 4. Ignoring stress is the best thing to do.

T (F) 5. Verbal aggression is a good way to handle stress.

(T) F 6. Talking with a trusted person outside the workplace can give a person insights into how to handle stress.

(T) F 7. Physical activity helps discharge negative feelings.

T (F) 8. Slamming doors and drawers at work will help discharge stress in a positive way.

(T) F 9. Writing a memo to the boss when you are angry is never a good idea.

T (F) 10. An angry response is an appropriate response to verbal aggression.

Check Your Understanding

1. Describe a situation that could cause stress.
   Sample response: Taking a test when you feel that you have not studied enough.

2. Describe two unacceptable responses to stress.
   Sample response: Yelling at someone, slamming doors.

3. Describe two acceptable responses to stress.
   Sample response: Talking with a friend, going for a walk.

4. How can a balanced life help you deal with stress?
   Sample response: When you spend time with friends, your attitude improves and you can be positive at work.

Rumors

DISCOVER

- the negative impact of rumors on the job.
- the role of attitude in the development and passing of rumors.
- how to avoid the rumor mill.

Case:
The Rumor Mill

Maria works for a local printer. An important shipment was late in arriving to one of the major customers. This customer was upset and threatened to find a new printer. Maria was asked to handle the problem.

Maria had not been on the job for long. She was surprised to get such an important assignment. It was exciting to face such a challenge. She used all her customer relations skills to come up with a solution that satisfied the customer. The customer relations manager, Lee, was happy with her performance.

"Maria," Lee says, "You did a wonderful job with that problem shipment. I had no doubt that you could handle it.

One rumor can negatively affect a large group of people.

DISCUSS

1. What is your reaction to this case?
   Sample responses: Maria should not be friends with Judith. Maria should ignore the others and concentrate on her job.

2. If you were Maria, what would you have done when you got the good news?
   Sample responses: I would have told my best friend at work. I would not have told anyone at work and let the supervisor make the announcement.

3. If you were Judith, what would you have done when you heard Maria's good news?
   Sample response: I would just have congratulated her and not said anything else.

4. If you were Maria, what would you have done when you heard the rumor?
   Sample responses: I would have ignored it. I would have started a new rumor saying we broke up.

I told the owner that you saved the account. There'll be a bonus in your paycheck. If you keep up the good work, I expect that within six months you'll be promoted to supervisor."

Maria can hardly believe her ears. She tells her coworker Judith her good news.

"I'm happy for you, Maria," Judith says, swallowing hard, "but don't get your hopes up about that promotion. Lee's buddy, Kwamie, told me he was sure he'd get that job. Everyone knows that Kwamie is next in line. If you'd been here longer, you'd know that Lee often makes promises he doesn't keep."

Maria feels completely deflated. Still, she resolves to do her best. As the months pass, she is given many major accounts. Lee often praises her performance.

Maria's only regret is that the friendships she has formed at the office are changing. Judith occasionally asks her to lunch, but the lunches feel like cross-examinations. Judith is constantly pumping her for information.

A few months later, Lee announces Maria's promotion to supervisor. Several times that week, all conversation stops when Maria enters the employee lounge. Maria decides to ask Judith what the problem is.

"What am I doing wrong, Judith? Do people really resent me that much? I'm only doing the best job I know how. I didn't try to take this promotion away from Kwamie. Do people think I badmouthed him? Is that the problem?"

Judith looks embarrassed. "Well, Maria, maybe I shouldn't tell you this, but the rumor is that you and Lee are dating. That's why you've been promoted, not Kwamie. Everyone thinks Lee is playing favorites."

Maria is shocked. "Judith, you know that's not true! Didn't you tell them the truth?"

Judith stammers, "What could I say? You told me yourself you thought Lee was very nice, and he clearly likes you a lot. What other reason could there be for your quick promotion?"

ANALYZE

Communication plays a key role in all human relations. It is natural to share information with others. When you spend several hours a day with coworkers, you often talk with them about your personal life, your family, and work. You talk about your joys and sorrows, successes and failures, hopes and fears. You also talk about information and news that you hear.

This sharing of information can have positive or negative results. Sharing can have negative results when the information passed on is incomplete or wrong. Often, the passing along of information turns into a rumor.

Rumors Usually Contain Misinformation

A **rumor** is information that people pass around, but no one knows where the information came from or whether the information is true. Rumors often spread in places where the same group of people meets every day, such as a school or a workplace. Usually, the topic of the rumor is of great interest to the group of people. Because so many people are interested in the topics of rumors, they spread quickly.

Even if the information in a rumor is correct at the start, it usually changes along the way. Each time a new person hears the rumor and passes it on, the new person may change the content slightly. Usually this changing is not done on purpose. The new person may just mishear or misunderstand what was said. Correct information may change into misinformation. **Misinformation** is untrue or incomplete information.

Rumors Are Spread by the Rumor Mill

How does information become misinformation? Worker *A* may overhear two supervisors talking about a possible layoff of one part-time worker. He repeats this information to Worker *B*. Worker *B* then repeats it to Worker *C*. By the time Worker *Z* hears the rumor, its content has become "Major layoffs will occur in every department."

The process just described is called the **rumor mill**. A rumor mill is a process in which people hear a rumor and pass it on. Information that goes through a rumor mill usually becomes misinformation. Some rumors may be partly true. Many are not true at all.

Rumors Negatively Affect Productivity

When workers hear a rumor such as, "Major layoffs will occur in every department," they become alarmed. They become worried that their jobs may be cut. Productivity declines as workers worry about their future. Workers bring that worry home with them and may begin losing sleep. One rumor can negatively affect a large group of people.

Rumors Negatively Affect Relationships

Maria's relationships with her coworkers were negatively affected by a rumor. They stopped talking to her and to each other in her presence. Maria's happiness in her new promotion was spoiled by the rumor mill.

The Rumor Mill Is Hard to Avoid

Maria made a couple of mistakes. She shared Lee's positive comments with the wrong person. Maria was unaware that Judith and Kwamie had been coworkers for a long time. Judith felt loyal to Kwamie. This loyalty may have affected her reaction to Maria's news, or maybe Judith was jealous of Maria's success. Either way, Judith couldn't wait to tell Kwamie what Maria had said. Kwamie, who wanted the promotion for himself, was upset. His status as the next in line for promotion was threatened. The rumor mill began to make up reasons for Maria's success.

Maria also discovered that Judith was not able to keep a secret. You have probably had a similar experience. You told a secret to someone who did not keep it secret. For most people, it is impossible to keep a secret. After your secret was out, you regretted ever having talked about it. You became angry and upset with the "friend" who betrayed your secret. At work, the best approach is simply this: If you do not want information to become common knowledge, do not share it with anyone.

Avoid Negative Comments

Avoid negative comments about others. Negative talk, like a negative attitude, is destructive. If you hear something, keep it to yourself. When you talk to coworkers, assume that everything you say will be repeated. Do not say anything that would be embarrassing if people knew about it.

Rumors often start with negative comments about coworkers, supervisors, or the company's future. The rumor mill is especially active when companies undergo change, for example, when a company is sold.

Be careful about "harmless rumors." Examine your reasons for telling someone something, especially something negative. "If you can't say something nice, don't say anything" is old advice, but still true. Think of the rumors you have heard—very few were positive.

Do Not Share Confidential Information

Be especially careful about **confidential information**. Confidential information is private information. Many businesses have confidential information that people within the company must know, but which they do not want people outside the company to know. This type of information is also called *trade secrets*.

Confidential information can also be private personal information. People who work in human resources have access to private personal information, such as social security numbers or health conditions. This information must be protected and kept private. Only designated people in the company are allowed access to this information. Administrative assistants may see such information as part of their job, and they must take care to keep that information private.

Gossip consists of rumors about the personal, private lives of

people. Many people love gossip, but gossip is often untrue. Even if the information starts out true, it goes through the rumor mill and becomes misinformation.

Do Not Believe Everything You Hear

When you hear negative comments, examine the motives of the person talking. **Motives** are the reasons that explain a person's actions. When Judith warned Maria not to get her hopes up about the promotion, what were her motives? Did she really want to warn Maria of a problem? Maybe she just wanted to say something to make Maria be less successful at work. Maybe her loyalty to Kwamie was leading her to say things that might discourage Maria.

Maria needed to examine Judith's comments about Lee in the same way. If Maria had accepted what Judith said about Lee, the negative comments might have undermined Maria's ability to work with Lee. If Maria started having problems working with Lee, her performance might have fallen. If her work became very poor, it might have cost her the promotion.

Do Not Spread Rumors

Employees with constructive attitudes are less likely to pass rumors. Loyalty to an employer will also make workers less likely to repeat things that may not be true. Repeating negative information (or worse—making it up) is destructive behavior. When you hear negative information, gossip, or rumors, change the subject. Discuss a hobby, sports, or a movie.

DISCUSS

1. What was Maria's attitude toward her job?
Maria's attitude was positive and constructive.

2. What was Judith's attitude toward her job?
Judith's attitude was negative, and she does not trust her boss.

3. Do you think Maria did anything wrong? Explain.
Sample responses: Yes, she should not be so friendly with Lee. No, she was only doing her best at her job; she deserved the promotion.

4. What was Judith's role in spreading the rumor?
Judith did nothing to stop the rumor.

5. Describe another way that Judith might have responded to Maria's news.
Sample response: Judith could just have congratulated Maria, without sharing office gossip.

APPLY

Case:
New Manager, Many Rumors

You have been happy with your job. You are good at what you do, the job is interesting and pays well, and you know what is expected of you every day. You worked well with your former manager, who left the company last month. You anticipate having the same good relationship with your new manager. However, you hear a rumor that the new manager plans to make sweeping changes in the organization of the department. You also hear that she is a horrible person to work for. Coworkers are hinting that it's time to start looking for a new job.

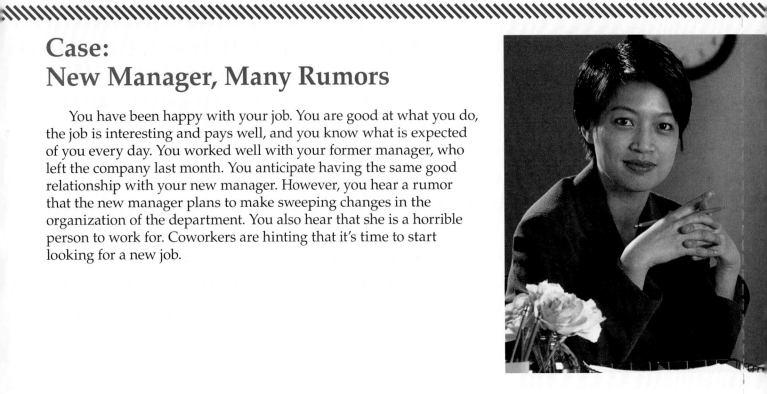

DISCUSS

1. List three options for dealing with your job situation.

   Option 1: **Sample response: You could panic and start looking for a new job.**

   Option 2: **Sample response: You could pass the rumor on and spend all your work time discussing the situation with coworkers.**

   Option 3: **Sample response: You could focus on doing your job and wait to see what the new manager does.**

2. List the option you would choose, and explain why you would choose it.
   Sample response: Option 3. It's a waste of time to worry about something that has not yet happened. So the best course is to continue working hard and wait to see what the new manager is really like.

REVIEW

True or False

Circle *T* if the statement is true or *F* if the statement is false.

T (F) 1. The sharing of information is always positive.

(T) F 2. A rumor is misinformation whose subject matter is of interest to others.

T (F) 3. Rumors are good because they keep employees informed of management decisions.

(T) F 4. One rumor can negatively affect a large group of people.

(T) F 5. Rumors may start out fairly accurate, but may change completely as they are spread.

(T) F 6. People who spread rumors often have negative motives.

(T) F 7. Confidential information ceases to be confidential if shared with someone who should not receive it.

T (F) 8. Employees with constructive attitudes are most likely to start rumors because they communicate well with others.

T (F) 9. The rumor mill can make a good job more fun.

(T) F 10. Negative talk is as destructive as negative attitudes.

Check Your Understanding

1. What is a rumor?
   Information that people pass around, but no one knows where the information came from or whether it is true.

2. When correct information goes through the rumor mill, how does it become misinformation?
   Someone may mishear or misunderstand the information; so when this person repeats the information, he or she gives misinformation.

3. How can a rumor cause a decrease in productivity?
   If workers hear a negative rumor, such as "major layoffs will occur," they may become alarmed and worry about their futures instead of working.

4. What can you do to avoid the rumor mill?
   Do not tell confidential information to anyone. Avoid negative comments. Change the subject when someone tries to tell you a rumor or negative information.

Topic 11

Accepting Responsibility

DISCOVER

- the importance of accepting responsibility for your actions.
- the importance of taking action to correct mistakes.

Case: The Tardy Worker

Amalie is an assistant in the marketing department of a magazine publishing company. Her work is good, and her boss likes her attitude. However, Amalie has trouble getting to work on time. On most days, she arrives a half-hour late, at 9:00 a.m. instead of 8:30 a.m. She says the reason is heavy traffic, and the bus she takes goes through construction.

Since she was a small child, Amalie has had difficulty getting started in the morning. She likes the evening and usually stays up late. She often goes to movies or parties. When she does not go out, she stays up late reading and watching television.

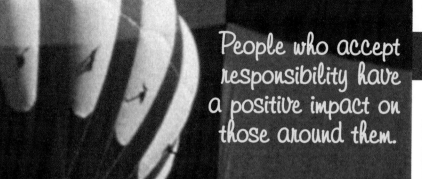

People who accept responsibility have a positive impact on those around them.

DISCUSS

1. What is your reaction to this case?

   Sample responses: Amalie is at fault; she should get to work on time. Shanice is too rigid; she should let Amalie get in whatever time she wants.

2. Describe Amalie's attitude toward work.

   Amalie's attitude toward work is basically good, but she is not responsible about getting to work on time.

3. Did Shanice help Amalie by allowing her to come in at a later hour?

   Sample responses: Yes, it showed Amalie that the arrival time did not matter. No, it just resulted in Amalie's getting to work later and later.

4. Describe what Amalie could have done to create a better outcome.

   Sample response: Amalie could have taken responsibility and gotten to work on time.

Shanice, Amalie's manager, calls her into her office. Shanice wants Amalie to be on time, but does not want to discourage her because her work is good. "It is not fair to the other employees," she explains. "They have already been working for a half hour by the time you get here."

Amalie has an idea. "What if I work half an hour later each day, with the understanding that I start half an hour later in the morning."

"Are you sure that will make a difference? Will you be able to get here by 9:00 a.m. sharp?" Shanice asks. Amalie says yes. They agree to the new schedule.

For two weeks, Amalie is at work every day at 9:00 a.m. sharp. Gradually, however, she starts coming in later until she regularly arrives at 9:20 or 9:30. She realizes that traffic is still bad at the later time and that getting up an hour later is no easier.

After six weeks, Shanice calls her into her office again. Amalie says, "I'm sorry. I really am trying. The traffic is even worse at the later hour. I think it will work better if I come in at 9:30 and leave at 5:30."

"Absolutely not," says Shanice. She points out that she has been willing to give Amalie six weeks to try the new schedule, but it did not work. "Now," she says, you must come in at 8:30 as do the others." Shanice makes a note in Amalie's personnel file to monitor her. She tells Amalie, "You may be put on probation if you continue to arrive late, and there will be no raises or promotion until you consistently arrive on time."

ANALYZE

Accepting responsibility is an important human relations skill. **Accepting responsibility** means being willing to answer for your actions and decisions. It also means being willing to accept the **consequences** (results) of your behavior. People who refuse to accept responsibility for their actions have a negative impact on those around them. At work, this affects both relationships and group productivity.

Don't Blame Others; Solve the Problem

People who are unwilling or unable to accept responsibility for their actions usually have poor human relations. People who do not accept responsibility often try to blame someone or something else. Here are some examples:

"No, I didn't finish the report. People kept interrupting me."

"I didn't do the job right because you didn't explain it clearly."

"I would have done it better if you had let me do it my way."

"I don't know what happened to it. It's just gone."

You can probably think of other examples. How do people who use these excuses make you feel? Are you eager to work with them? People who cannot take responsibility for their actions annoy their coworkers. Soon, others may shun them too.

If someone on the team does not take responsibility for his or her actions, how does that affect the team? Not taking responsibility may result in work not being completed on time. Missing deadlines reduces team productivity. The blaming does not solve the problem. In a work setting, making excuses or blaming others is not acceptable. If you have a problem, you should consult with your teammates or your supervisor and solve the problem.

Know Yourself

To accept responsibility often requires a sound knowledge of yourself. You need to be able to assess your own strengths and weaknesses. For example, Amalie blamed the traffic for her lateness. If she had looked at herself honestly, she would have realized that she was not accepting her

responsibility to get to work on time. She has a constant problem with getting up in the morning. She needs to solve this personal problem, not blame traffic. Everyone deals with traffic, but only Amalie is always late to work.

Accepting responsibility does not mean that you have to accept blame or go around confessing. It does require you to know yourself. It requires that you think about what type of person you want to be and make adjustments to meet your goals. Amalie needs to find a way to get to work on time, or she will not be able to hold a normal office job.

If you cannot change your shortcomings, you will need to adjust your life accordingly. Amalie could explore jobs that start later in the day, although she might still have trouble getting to work then. She could also think about working for herself, so she could set her own hours.

Admit Mistakes and Correct Them

Accepting responsibility is closely related to another human relations skill: the ability to admit a mistake. It is easy to accept responsibility when things go well. The person with good human relations skills is able to accept responsibility when things go wrong. Doing so is good human relations because people respect and admire people who admit mistakes.

However, accepting responsibility for problems or mistakes is not much good if you do nothing. You must follow through to correct the mistake or solve the problem. Accepting responsibility is the first step toward correcting whatever the problem might be, but it is only a first step. You must use all your human relations skills to work with your team and supervisor to correct the mistake and prevent it from happening again.

DISCUSS

1. How does Amalie manage to avoid the consequences of her lateness?
Amalie's work is good, so her boss lets her get in later.

2. Did Shanice help Amalie by allowing her to come in at a later hour?
Not really. Allowing Amalie to come in later did not help Amalie solve her problem with getting to work on time.

3. What would you have done if you had been Amalie's supervisor?
Sample response: I would have demanded that Amalie get in on time at the same time as everyone else. If she could not do so, she would be fired.

4. What advice would you give to Amalie?
Sample response: Go to bed earlier and get up earlier, or find a different job.

APPLY

Case:
Someone Else's Mistake

You are given an important report to complete and send to the printer by Friday. You are anxious to complete the report and get it printed on Thursday because you have plans to take Friday off for vacation. Unfortunately, some information you need is delayed. By the time it arrives and the report is finished, it is late Thursday afternoon. A coworker offers to drop off the report at the printer for you on Friday, and you gratefully accept.

When you pick up the report from the printer on Monday, you are stunned to discover that it is printed in black ink, not colored ink. Your coworker misunderstood the instructions and gave the wrong information to the printer. There is no way the report can be redone on time. You are not looking forward to explaining the mix-up to your boss.

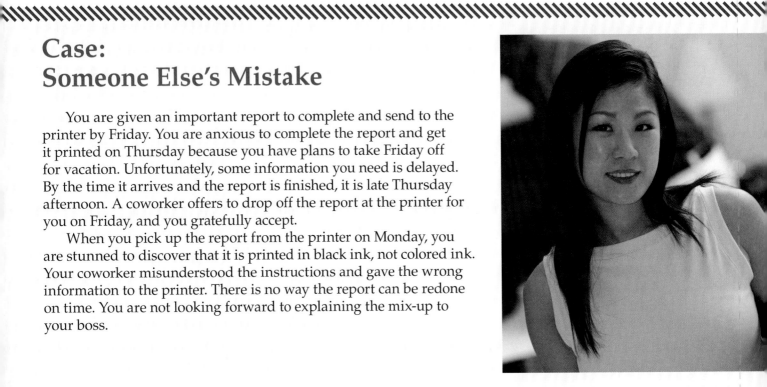

DISCUSS

1. List three options for dealing with your job situation.

    Option 1: __Sample response: Blame the printer._____

    _____

    Option 2: __Sample response: Blame your coworker._____

    _____

    Option 3: __Sample response: Take responsibility for your actions.____

    _____

2. List the option you would choose, and explain why you would choose it.
    __Sample response: Option 3. The project was your responsibility, not your coworker's, so it was__
    __your fault that a mistake was made._____

    _____

REVIEW

True or False

Circle *T* if the statement is true or *F* if the statement is false.

(T) F 1. When team members accept responsibility for their actions, the team is usually more productive.

(T) F 2. What a person fails to do is often as important as what the person actually does.

(T) F 3. People who have an excuse for everything are failing to accept responsibility.

T (F) 4. Admitting a mistake is a serious error on the job.

(T) F 5. Accepting responsibility requires self-knowledge.

T (F) 6. A responsible person tries to hide his or her mistakes.

T (F) 7. Accepting responsibility means a person should confess his or her weaknesses to others.

(T) F 8. If a worker has difficulty meeting a job's requirements, he or she can look for a more suitable job.

(T) F 9. Accepting responsibility when the consequences are negative is a constructive human relations skill.

T (F) 10. People look down on those who admit their mistakes.

Check Your Understanding

1. In your own words, explain how accepting responsibility for one's actions is a human relations skill.
   Sample response: Accepting responsibility makes human interactions go more smoothly and helps work teams be more productive.

2. Describe an action and its consequence.
   Sample response: Studying for a test results in getting a good grade.

3. How can blaming others reduce team productivity?
   If you blame others, the problem does not get solved and the team may miss a deadline.

4. Why is just admitting a mistake not enough?
   If you just admit a mistake, the mistake is still there. You must take action to correct the mistake and keep it from happening again.

Part 3
Succeeding on
the Job

Topic 12

Communication

DISCOVER

- how good communication skills help you build positive relationships at work.
- how a positive attitude helps you be an effective communicator.
- how nonverbal communication affects messages.

Case: The Very Bad, Terrible, Horrible First Day

An insurance company has a small medical benefits department. This department processes claims for more than 15,000 employees. The insurance claims adjusters have to fill in several forms for each claim. They have to make sure payment checks are requested for doctors, hospitals, and labs. Every worker in the department has too much to do.

Tyrone arrives on Monday morning feeling stressed. His desk is piled high with past-due claims. On top of that, he will have to begin training Emma, a new employee. Tyrone is sure this will be a terrible week.

Career success depends on good communication.

DISCUSS

Tyrone is deep into his work on a complicated claim when Emma arrives. He looks up at her with a loud sigh. She says hello, and he gives her a brief nod. She sees that he seems annoyed at the interruption. He sits at his desk, stares at Emma, and waits for her to talk. He taps his pencil impatiently.

Emma, already anxious about the new job, fills the silence with nervous chatter about her previous job experience. Finally, Tyrone leans back in his chair, arms folded, and says, "I'm very busy today. I was asked to train you, and I will; but I don't want to know your life's history."

Emma is embarrassed. When she arrived, she was sure of herself. She thought she would make a good first impression. Now Tyrone acts as if she is a nuisance. In a whisper, with reddened cheeks, Emma says, "I'm very sorry. I didn't mean to waste your time."

Tyrone looks down at his desk and moves some papers around without answering. He hands Emma paper and a pen and proceeds to list her tasks. She writes very fast, but she can't keep up with his pace. He doesn't seem to notice. He jumps from topic to topic without stopping. When she interrupts to ask questions, his look tells her that she is brainless for not understanding. Emma's self-confidence is fading.

Several times during the training session, the phone rings. Tyrone answers with a short "Yes?" and abruptly ends the calls. "At least," Emma thinks, "it's not just me."

As the morning progresses, Emma feels more and more lost. She tries to tell Tyrone, but he is not listening. He avoids eye contact with her.

At the beginning of her first day, Emma was smiling. She was a bit nervous but excited. She was looking forward to starting a new job and meeting new people. As she leaves at the end of the day, her shoulders are hunched and her head is down. The excitement is gone.

1. Describe how Tyrone communicated verbally.
   Sample response: Tyrone tells Emma that he is busy and that he does not want to know her life's history. His words have a negative tone.

2. Describe how Tyrone communicated nonverbally.
   Sample response: Tyrone taps his pencil, speaks fast, and avoids eye contact.

3. What role did Tyrone's attitude play in his communication with Emma?
   Tyrone's negative attitude resulted in his negative behavior toward Emma.

4. Do you think Tyrone and Emma can build a good relationship after their first meeting?
   Sample responses: It seems unlikely because Tyrone is the boss and he is so negative. They might build a good relationship if Tyrone takes the first step and works at it.

ANALYZE

Communication is the heart of good human relations. Communication and attitude go hand in hand. The way you communicate sends messages about your attitude. Your attitude affects how you communicate. Both are keys to success in personal and work relationships. Productivity falls when workers cannot communicate and get along. The best product in the world may go unsold if the seller cannot communicate with the buyer. The most needed service may not be used if the attitude of the service provider is poor.

Communication skills are often divided into two types: verbal communication and nonverbal communication.

Verbal Communication

Verbal communication consists of using words to send messages. Verbal communication includes speaking, writing, reading, and listening. Words provide us with a precise way to communicate a message. The clarity of the message depends on three things: your choice of words, your use of grammar, and how you organize your thoughts.

Your attitude can affect how well you choose your words and organize your thoughts. Tyrone was absorbed in his own problems. He had too much to do and had fallen behind. He felt negative about training Emma. As a result of his negative attitude, his choice of words conveyed his negative attitude: "I'm very busy today. I was asked to train you, and I will; but I don't want to know your life's history."

Nonverbal Communication

Nonverbal communication consists of everything you communicate *without* words. It includes hand gestures, facial expressions, posture, and position. Nonverbal communication is often called body language, but it also includes tone of voice and speed of speaking.

Tyrone's negative attitude was expressed in his body language, as well as his words. He avoided eye contact with Emma, tapped his pencil, and spoke too fast. Such behaviors are even clearer than spoken words. Their

message to Emma was, "You annoy me, and I don't want to deal with you."

Being aware of your body language is key to good communication. Think about the simple act of not smiling when you meet someone. If the person is your friend, he or she might ask, "What's wrong?" If the person is a new acquaintance, he or she might think "not friendly" or "doesn't like me."

On the job, you have to be aware of what you are saying with your gestures, facial expressions, and tone of voice, as well as your words.

Listening

Communication is a two-way street. Getting your message across is one part; listening to the other person is the rest. What happens when two people talk at the same time? They don't hear each other. Likewise, if you are too busy listening to your own thoughts, you cannot hear the other person.

The goal of communication is to establish a relationship with another person. To do this, you need to hear what the other person is saying. Stop and listen to the actual words. Be aware of the other person's nonverbal cues. If you're explaining something, notice if the person nods but also frowns. A frown can mean you are not being understood. You might need to stop and ask if there are any questions.

When someone else is speaking, show that you are listening. Make eye contact. Nod your head. Hold up a hand if you want the person to stop so you can ask a question; or simply interrupt and say, "Excuse

me, I have a question." Letting someone go on and on when you don't understand might seem polite. However, leading someone to think you understand when you don't can backfire. Listening carefully and responding honestly is a part of being a good communicator.

Communication and Your Attitude

Tyrone's poor attitude toward training Emma was evident through his verbal and nonverbal communication. Emma felt a little better when she saw that Tyrone was rude to everyone. However, by the end of the day, Tyrone's negative attitude had affected Emma. She no longer felt positive about her new job. If Tyrone's negative attitude continues, it will not inspire Emma to work hard and do her best. If Tyrone were less stressed, he would welcome an eager worker who is willing to shoulder some of the overload.

Tyrone forgot that his job involved people as well as paperwork. He was asked to train a new person because he was good at his job. What will happen when his supervisor finds out that Emma didn't learn very much on her first day? What will the supervisor think about Tyrone's ability to take on new job roles?

Much of your career success depends on how well you communicate. Good communication skills and good human relations skills go hand in hand. Your attitude influences the way you communicate. The way you communicate with others affects their opinion of you and their attitude toward you.

DISCUSS

1. What words did Tyrone use to show his annoyance?
"I'm very busy…I don't want to know your life's history."

2. Give examples of nonverbal communication that Tyrone used to show his annoyance.
Sample response: A loud sigh, staring at her, tapping his pencil, and speaking too fast.

3. What role did Tyrone's attitude play in his communication with Emma?
Tyrone's negative attitude interfered with his ability to communicate with Emma.

4. How can you tell that Emma's attitude had changed?
At the end of the day, Emma's shoulders were hunched and her head was down.

5. Do you think Tyrone and Emma can form a good working relationship after this first encounter?
Sample response: If both Tyrone and Emma work at it, their relationship might improve. However, unless a third party intervenes, it is unlikely that their communication will improve.

APPLY

Case: Face-to-Face vs. Electronic Communication

You are confident in your communication skills. You enjoy meeting clients and customers and have little problem communicating face-to-face. Lately, however, budget cutbacks have required you to do more work over the telephone and by e-mail. Your sales are off, even though you are dealing with the same people.

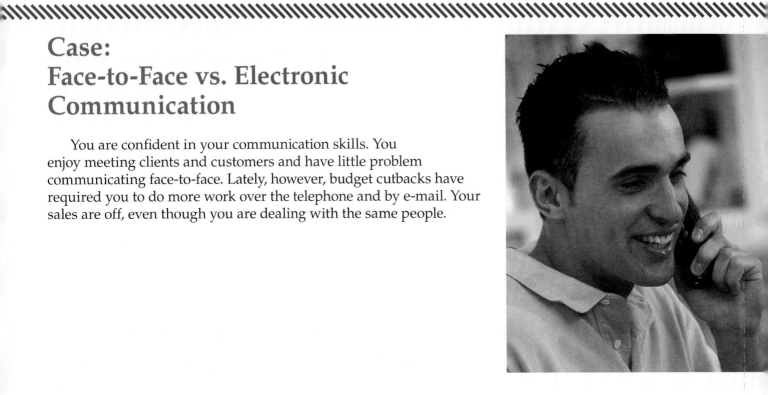

DISCUSS

1. What might be the cause of this problem?
   Sample responses: You may not be very effective in using the phone or in writing. You may rely a great deal on nonverbal communication, and nonverbal communication is less apparent over the phone and not apparent at all in e-mail.

2. What can you do to solve the problem?
   Sample responses: On the phone, smile when you speak. Even though the other person cannot see you, a smile will make your tone of voice friendlier. Practice phone calls with a friend or colleague who can give you good feedback. Have someone read and critique your e-mails.

REVIEW

True or False

Circle *T* if the statement is true or *F* if the statement is false.

T (F) 1. Attitude has no affect on how a person communicates.

T (F) 2. Verbal communication refers to spoken words only.

(T) F 3. Word choice affects how clear you message is.

T (F) 4. Nonverbal communication cannot take place over the telephone.

(T) F 5. Attitude toward others can be conveyed by tone of voice.

T (F) 6. Nonverbal communication is less important than verbal communication.

(T) F 7. Listening is part of communication.

(T) F 8. Listeners can convey their attitude toward a speaker by their body language.

T (F) 9. Nonverbal communication skills are *not* relevant to career success.

(T) F 10. Sometimes a nonverbal message is stronger than a verbal message.

Check Your Understanding

1. Give an example of verbal communication.
   <u>Sample responses: Saying hello, saying "I'm glad to see you," sending a written letter or</u>
   <u>e-mail, making and showing a film or video.</u>

2. Give an example of nonverbal communication.
   <u>Sample responses: Waving hello, frowning, smiling, and shaking hands.</u>

3. Give an example of how attitude affects communication.
   <u>Sample response: When people have a negative attitude, they are likely to choose negative</u>
   <u>words to communicate, and their body language shows their irritation with others.</u>

4. Explain why listening is an important part of communication.
   <u>The goal of communication is to establish a relationship. To establish a relationship, you have</u>
   <u>to hear and understand what the other person is saying.</u>

Topic 13

Your Attitude and Job Success

DISCOVER

- how to learn through observation.
- traits that form a constructive attitude.
- the role of a constructive attitude in career success.

Case: Learning by Observing

Jacob is one of the top sales representatives for a local printer. Because of his good performance, he is assigned to train Katie. Katie is the newest member of the sales team. She is looking forward to learning Jacob's secrets of success.

Katie is surprised when she first meets Jacob. She had expected to meet an outgoing, aggressive salesperson. She thought he would be self-assured and maybe even a bit pushy. Jacob is self-assured, but soft-spoken. He has a relaxed and gentle manner.

What Katie learns from Jacob is also surprising. Jacob has no high-powered pushy way of selling. He loves the

Integrity and initiative will put you on the path to success.

DISCUSS

1. Describe Jacob's attitude toward his job.

   Jacob has a positive and constructive attitude towards his job. He goes the extra mile to help his customers.

2. Why do Jacob's clients like him?

   Because he is calm and solves problems.

3. What do you think Katie is learning from Jacob?

   Sample response: How to be responsible, solve problems, and be calm.

company's products. He is sure his company has the best quality services and good prices. He sees his job as a chance to help others obtain the best service.

Jacob and Katie go on several sales calls. The customers seem happy to see Jacob. Katie notices that Jacob knows quite a lot about each business and its needs. He is able to suggest just the right product or service. He never fails to ask if his clients were pleased with their last order.

One day a problem arises. A large shipment is delayed. Unfortunately, it is one of Jacob's new accounts. The owner, Brian, is upset. He takes out his anger on Jacob. Katie expects Jacob to place the blame where it belongs, on the shipping department. However, Jacob apologizes without making excuses. He tracks down the lost shipment and delivers it himself that day. Brian realizes that he has treated Jacob unfairly. He is impressed with Jacob's calm and competent response. He tells Jacob that he will give his company another chance.

Katie trains with Jacob for a month. On several days, she

notices he seems quieter than usual. When she asks what is bothering him, Jacob tells her that his apartment building is being converted to condos, and he has to move. He is worried about finding another affordable apartment on short notice. Katie admires his ability to do his job when faced with personal problems. His clients are never aware that Jacob has anything on his mind but their needs.

ANALYZE

You can learn many things from a successful coworker. The manager chose Jacob to train Katie, the newest member of the sales team. The manager sees qualities in Jacob that he would like all employees to have.

Observational Learning

Katie watched Jacob closely. She listened and observed how he handled relationships. She learned from observing his behavior. Watching someone to learn how to do something is called **observational learning**. It can be especially helpful when you start a new job.

When you learn by observing others, look for the attitudes and behaviors that make them successful. Then work to incorporate those attitudes and behaviors into your attitudes and behaviors. To learn by observing, follow these steps:

- Carefully watch the person as he or she does the job.
- Ask questions.
- Picture the behavior in your mind.
- Remember what was said.
- Practice using the behavior you have observed.

Katie's personality differs from Jacob's. She is bubbly and outgoing, while he is calm and quiet. However, she can learn many constructive attitudes and useful behaviors from him. For example, she can learn not to blame others for mistakes, but instead to work quickly to solve the problem.

Traits of Valued Employees

A person's attitude is noticed by others, especially employers. They try to hire people with a constructive attitude. Some of the traits that contribute to a constructive attitude are dependability, loyalty, honesty, and conscientiousness. A person with these traits has **integrity** (good character).

Dependability is the quality of doing what you say you will do and fulfilling your promises. When you are dependable, customers know they can count on you to do what you say you will do. You will provide the products and services that you promise. Coworkers know you will do your share on the job, not let tasks fall to them.

Loyalty is the quality of being faithful to someone or something. Loyalty includes *not* doing anything to harm that person or his or her reputation. Loyalty to your company means that you will not make negative comments about the company and its products. Loyalty to coworkers means that you will not contribute to the rumor mill. You will not gossip or make fun of coworkers behind their backs.

If you have a problem with your supervisor, loyalty to that person's position requires you to take your problem directly to him or her. Talking to others first shows disloyalty.

Honesty is the quality of telling the truth and *not* stealing. Telling the truth is very important in a work setting. Your coworkers and supervisor have to know that the information you give them about the progress of a project is accurate. Your customers need to trust that the information you give them is true.

Stealing any items from an employer is dishonest. Stealing time is also dishonest. Ten minutes late in the morning, running out to buy coffee, fifteen minutes late from lunch—all these minutes add up to time away from work and reduced productivity. Receiving or making personal phone calls is another theft of time. Personal use of the copy machine and company supplies is also viewed as stealing.

Conscientiousness is the quality of being committed to doing what is right and proper. The conscientious worker performs well, whether supervised or not. Conscientious employees have good relationships because supervisors and coworkers know they will do their jobs properly and *not* make excuses for mistakes.

Initiative

In addition to integrity, a worker needs initiative. **Initiative** is the quality of self-motivation, the ability to get the job done on your own. Initiative is what separates a positive attitude from a constructive attitude.

An employee with initiative does not wait to be told what to do. He or she sees what is needed and takes action. The administrative assistant with initiative enrolls in a computer course to learn a new computer program. When the new program is installed on her computer, she will be ready to use it.

Along with initiative comes the need for good judgment. You wouldn't want to do anything that is not authorized by your supervisor. Nor would you want to make decisions without notifying your supervisor or coworkers. Knowing how far to go on your own and when to seek permission is a matter of judgment. This is where observational learning comes in. Observing your workplace, especially your supervisor and successful coworkers, will help you develop good judgment.

Jacob's company is lucky to have him as a sales representative. His personal qualities and constructive attitude are an asset to the business. Try to imagine Jacob being consistently late for work or failing to show for an appointment. Can you picture him joining in gossip about another employee or complaining about his company to a customer? Jacob's human relations skills will take him far.

DISCUSS

1. List three things Katie can learn from Jacob.
   Sample responses: Dependability, loyalty, honesty, conscientiousness, and initiative.
2. Why is observational learning often better than book learning?
   Sample response: You can see how a process is actually done.
3. How do dependability, loyalty, honesty, and conscientiousness contribute to a constructive attitude?
   These qualities give a person the reasons to take action on behalf of others. Taking action is an important part of a constructive attitude.
4. Why is initiative important?
   Initiative is the motivation for taking action. Taking action is part of a constructive attitude.

APPLY

Case: How to Bring Costs Down

Your department has been informed that it has gone over its budget. The telephone bills are over budget due to more calls. The office supplies are over budget due to increased usage of paper products, including photocopy paper.

There is no obvious explanation for these problems, such as an increase in business. In fact, it is the slow season and business has decreased for the past two months. The supervisor calls the staff together to talk about how costs can be brought down.

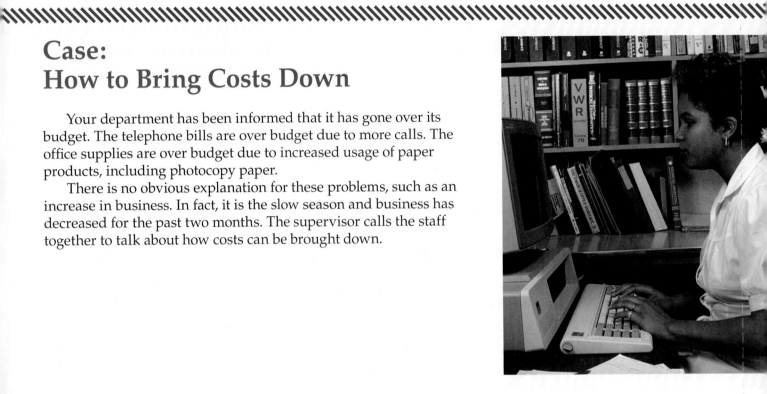

DISCUSS

1. List three suggestions to bring costs down.
   Sample response: Monitor usage of office supplies and the number of phone calls. Have a contest for the person who offers the best suggestion for reducing costs. Explore new vendors for supplies; another vendor might have the same supplies for a lower cost.

2. How might an "employee of the month" program help bring costs down?
   Reward employees who find ways to lower costs. Then share those ways with everyone else.

3. List five qualities that the employee who wins "employee of the month" should have.
   Dependability, honesty, loyalty, conscientiousness, and initiative.

REVIEW

True or False

Circle *T* if the statement is true or *F* if the statement is false.

(T) F   1. Observational learning is helpful when a person starts a new job.

T (F) 2. Dependability is only important in relationships with customers.

(T) F   3. Loyalty is one of the reasons employees should avoid contributing to the rumor mill.

(T) F   4. Making personal phone calls is a form of stealing from the company.

(T) F   5. Taking long coffee breaks is a form of stealing from the company.

T (F) 6. Most businesses expect their employees to take home office supplies.

T (F) 7. Conscientious workers need close supervision.

T (F) 8. In the work world, being a good person is enough to get ahead.

(T) F   9. An employee with initiative must also use good judgment.

(T) F 10. Integrity, initiative, and a constructive attitude are the marks of a valuable employee.

Check Your Understanding

1. Describe how observational learning works.
   You watch someone performing a task, then you try to do the same task.

2. List four traits that contribute to integrity.
   Dependability, loyalty, honesty, and conscientiousness.

3. Describe initiative.
   Initiative is taking action based on good judgment.

Topic 14

Strategies for a Positive Attitude

DISCOVER

- the three components of work attitude.
- ten strategies for improving your work attitude.

Case:
Staying Positive

Mardryka is a nurse's aide at a local nursing home. She works the evening shift, from 3 p.m. to 11 p.m. She usually arrives 15 minutes early for her shift. Those extra minutes give her time to talk to the aide from the previous shift. She can find out whether any of the patients on her floor are having difficulty. Sometimes, patient problems during the day mean that some of the duties of the day shift have to be handled in the evening. Today is one of those days. Mardryka receives a quick briefing and plans how she will organize her time to fit in everything that needs to be done.

As Mardryka enters the hall, Eileen calls to her. Mardryka waves hello, but keeps on walking. Eileen, the senior aide

Focus on the positive.

DISCUSS

1. Describe Mardryka's attitude toward her job.
   Mardryka's attitude is positive and constructive.

2. Describe Eileen's attitude toward her job.
   Eileen's attitude is negative; she does not want to be there.

3. What does Mardryka do to keep a positive attitude under difficult situations?
   Mardryka understands the causes of the patients' difficulties; this understanding helps her stay positive. She also does not take the patients' behavior personally.

on the evening shift, always has a complaint. As Mardryka walks down the hall, Eileen catches up with her.

"It's just you and me again tonight," Eileen says. "That darn Zachary called. One of his kids has the flu, and he can't take her to the sitter's. I'm getting sick and tired of this! I'll bet it's just an excuse to stay home and watch TV. I'll tell you…"

Mardryka cuts her short, trying to keep the irritation out of her voice. "Zachary hardly ever takes time off, Eileen. Why would you doubt his excuse? It's hard raising three young kids alone, and I admire him for working so hard to support them. Besides, the flu can be dangerous to an elderly person. Zachary should stay home rather than take the chance of spreading infection."

"Just makes more work for us," Eileen grumbles.

Mardryka starts the evening routine. Her patients are glad to see her. She always greets them pleasantly. When she has the time, she spends a few extra minutes chatting with them. Mardryka knows that many of these people rarely have visitors.

Conversation and attention are important to them.

Some patients are ill and in pain. Some have problems with memory. At times, a patient yells at an aide. Mardryka sometimes hears Eileen yell back. Mardryka realizes that the patients' anger is not directed at her personally. She knows they are angry at their illness and their inability to cope. Mardryka tries to put herself in their place. She treats all her patients as she would want to be treated.

Latoya is the registered nurse in charge on the evening shift. Latoya spends part of every evening checking Eileen's work, even though Eileen is the senior aide. However, Latoya knows that Mardryka will take care of what needs to be done without direct supervision.

Latoya considers Mardryka "her right arm." She often tells her, "I don't know what I would do without you." Mardryka has volunteered to attend in-service training sessions on her own time. She has asked to borrow Latoya's nursing journals. Latoya is encouraging Mardryka to attend nursing school.

ANALYZE

Everyone's life—home, school, work, and social—is full of ups and downs. It is normal to feel positive at some times and negative at others. How can you stay positive at work? First, understand what makes up your work attitudes. Then develop ways to help you maintain a positive work attitude.

Work Attitudes

Your **work attitude** has three components: attitude toward self, attitude toward work, and attitude toward the workplace.

Attitude Toward Self

The way you feel about yourself has a major effect on how you feel about work. Attitude toward self is often called **self-esteem**. When your self-esteem is high, you feel good about yourself. You are **self-confident**. You know you can handle any task that comes your way.

Your level of self-esteem affects how you deal with people and situations. When your self-esteem is high, you can see other people as equals and coworkers, not threats. It is easier to sympathize and understand what others are feeling. When your self-esteem is low, you tend to see other people as threats. You might not be able to sympathize with others or be understanding.

Think about Eileen's and Mardryka's responses to Zachary's absence. Mardryka's self-esteem enabled her to defend Zachary. Why? She doesn't need to put down another person to feel good about herself because she already feels good about herself.

As a result, she is able to see another person's side of things. She gives Zachary the benefit of the doubt and believes his reason for being absent. She also thinks about the welfare of the patients. Being exposed to the flu would be bad for them. Instead of being angry about doing more work, she feels good about filling in for Zachary.

Attitude Toward Work

A person's attitude toward work is often called his or her **work ethic**. People with a good work ethic feel that work is important. They want to get their work done on time and at a high quality. They don't expect work to always be easy. They get satisfaction from doing a good job, and they feel that the work itself is rewarding. People with a good work ethic are willing to pitch in when problems arise and are willing to put in extra hours when asked.

When Eileen heard that Zachary was not coming in, she was angry. She did not want to do any extra work. Eileen dislikes her work. Her work ethic is poor.

Attitude Toward the Workplace

Attitude toward the workplace means how you feel about the company or organization you work for. A positive attitude means that you respect the organization and the people who work there. You respect the company's products and are proud to tell people about your work.

Latoya could tell that Mardryka had a positive attitude toward the nursing home. She knew that Mardryka was committed to the nursing home's professional goal of serving elderly people. She saw that Mardryka cared about the patients and gave of herself. Doing the job means more to Mardryka than just earning a paycheck.

No job is perfect, and every job has its ups and downs. It is never easy to be positive all the time. The following are ten strategies that many people use to maintain a positive attitude.

1. Examine Your Attitude Regularly

Think about your day at work. Think about your relationships with your coworkers and supervisors. Is your attitude positive or negative? constructive or destructive?

If your attitude is negative, try to determine why. Ask yourself these questions:

- Am I unsuited for my job?
- Are personal problems interfering with my work performance?
- Do I dislike my coworkers or supervisor?
- Do I need more training to perform my tasks effectively?
- How can I change destructive attitudes to constructive ones?

If your attitude is positive, are you projecting that attitude to others? Most likely, you will discover one or two areas where you need to adjust your attitude. Ask yourself these questions:

- How would my supervisor describe me?
- How would my coworkers rate my human relations skills?

You may love your job but find that certain people or tasks cause you problems. When you find a problem, you can work to fix it.

2. Balance Work with Personal Life

All work and no play is not healthy, but all play and no work is not good either. Only you can decide how to allocate your time and energy. Figure out a balance that works for you. Decide on your **priorities**. When you know your priorities, it is easier to make the decisions that are right for you.

When you are at home, focus on your family and friends. Leave work problems at work. Similarly, when at work, put home problems on a back burner. Focus on your work. If you do not feel stressed about your priorities, it is easier to maintain a positive attitude toward work.

3. Focus on the Positive

If one aspect of your job gets you down, don't let it overshadow the positive aspects. Mardryka did not enjoy working with cranky patients. However, when her patients were irritable, she tried to make them feel better. Her focus was on the good she could do each day. She used her skills to make others feel better. It gave her satisfaction when they greeted her warmly. She felt that putting up with the occasional cranky patient was worth all the times when she felt good about her job.

Focus on the positive in your work and in your relationships on the job. Remember, you can have good working relationships with everyone, even with those who differ from you in many ways. Focus on the values and goals you share, such as building a productive department.

4. Communicate

Communication is your link with others. When you feel isolated at home or at work, your lines of communication need to be repaired. It's hard to keep a positive attitude if you feel misunderstood.

Practice good listening and communication skills every day. Be sure that you say what you

DISCUSS

1. How does high self-esteem help Mardryka have a positive attitude at work? **She does not need to put someone else down in order to feel good; she already feels good and knows that she is competent.**

2. What advice would you give to Eileen to help her improve her attitude toward work? **Sample response: Get more training, understand why your patients react as they do, and take some continuing education classes.**

(Continued)

ANALYZE

mean and that you hear what others are saying. Ask questions if you do not understand something. When you give directions, make sure your listeners understand you. Ask them to repeat your instructions back to you or to explain what you just told them.

5. Turn Unexpected Changes into Opportunity

Human beings are creatures of habit. It is the rare person who likes, suprises. We are comfortable with the familiar—friends, supervisors, coworkers, routines, foods. However, change is an inevitable part of life. If you stay in a job long enough, some unforeseen changes are sure to happen. Companies are bought and sold. Managers and coworkers come and go. Your duties change. New company policies go into effect.

Your first reaction to changes at work may be negative. You might not like a new boss or a new assignment. However, you can learn to accept change and remain positive. Focus on what you can learn. Be honest if something is bothering you, and talk to your supervisor about it. Every new situation can be a learning experience if you are open to learning. What you might learn is how to adapt to something you don't like. Adopt the attitude that every change presents a new **opportunity** to grow.

6. Educate Yourself

It's tough to be positive if you are having trouble doing your

job. Education is the key to being confident about your abilities. You can take courses to keep up with your field. You can read articles and new books by experts in the field. Mardryka pursued her education in both ways, by taking in-service training and by reading nursing journals.

Education is necessary for advancement in many careers. Even if that is not the case, education is never wasted. Be a lifelong learner. The more you learn, the more confident you will be.

7. Maintain Your Interest

In the first months on a job, you are learning new things. The excitement and challenge

keep you interested, and your attitude is positive.

As time goes on, you might begin to feel bored. You might feel that you are not being challenged, or that the work is not as much fun as you expected. If this happens, look for ways to regain the interest you once felt. Analyze your job duties. Look for areas where you can take more initiative. Come up with new ideas for doing routine tasks.

Supervisors count on workers with initiative and enthusiasm to show new employees the ropes. If Latoya were looking for an employee to train a newly hired aide, would she ask Mardryka or Eileen? Eileen may be the senior aide, but she no longer has any enthusiasm for her job. Her negative attitude affects her

relationships with the patients, supervisors, and other aides.

8. Maintain a Sense of Humor

Humor can help your outlook on almost anything. Taking yourself and others too seriously will not solve problems. It may cause you to dwell on mistakes or focus on the negative side of situations that cannot be changed. Having a sense of humor does *not* mean joking or clowning around. Having a sense of humor means developing the ability to see the lighter side of situations. People with a good sense of humor can say just the right thing to make everyone laugh and break the tension. Find someone with a good sense of humor, and learn by observation.

9. Take Care of Your Health

Poor health habits can affect your job performance and your attitude. The negative effects of poor health habits might not happen immediately; but over time, such habits can reduce your productivity on the job. An occasional candy bar for lunch will not ruin your health, but a steady diet of junk food will sap your energy.

Staying up too late every night will affect your ability to be alert the next day. A lack of exercise may result in a buildup of tensions and lack of energy. Abuse of alcohol and drugs will impair your ability to perform. In most workplaces, use of alcohol or any illegal substances on the job is grounds for immediate dismissal.

10. Dress for Success

Your attitude and your appearance are related. If you look good, you are more likely to feel good about yourself. Everyone has a favorite outfit that can improve a mood instantly. Choose clothes that make you feel good about yourself.

Your appearance also affects others' opinions of you and their reactions to you. Be aware of the dress code for your job. Pay attention to personal hygiene and grooming.

A supervisor might make decisions about your future based on how you dress and your grooming. He or she may or may not ever mention this to you. The supervisor may not even be aware of how your hygiene and grooming affect his or her opinions of you. It is up to you to show your feelings about yourself, your position, and your workplace by presenting an appropriate image.

DISCUSS

3. Give an example to illustrate each of the strategies.
   Sample response: 1. I have started getting to work late. I can ask myself if there is a problem at work and try to solve the problem. 2. I have dinner with my friends every Friday. 3. I don't like filing, but I enjoy all the other parts of my job, so I focus on them. 4. When my boss gives me instructions, I let her know if I don't understand. 5. I have been given a new assignment and have to work with new people; I am keeping a positive attitude. 6. I am taking a continuing education course. 7. I was getting bored at work, so I volunteered for a new project. 8. Everyone was getting discouraged, so I told a funny story about how everyone makes mistakes. 9. I bring an apple for a snack every day. 10. I wear a suit every day, even though my job does not require it.

APPLY

Case:
Torn Between Two Priorities

You are in competition for a promotion at work. At the same time, your family is moving to a new home. Your boss keeps asking you to come in on Saturdays to help with a special project. Your family is counting on you to organize the move and help pack. You are exhausted because of the physical and mental demands that are being placed on you. You are torn between your need to spend time at home and your desire to advance.

DISCUSS

1. List three options for dealing with your job situation.
   Option 1: **Sample response: Ignore the stress and keep on trying to meet the demands of work and family.**

   Option 2: **Sample response: Make your career your top priority and put most of your time and energy into your career.**

   Option 3: **Sample response: Make your family your top priority and put most of your time and energy into your family.**

2. List the option you would choose, and explain why you would choose it.
   Strike a balance between Options 2 and 3. Working extra hours for a special purpose is fine. Over the long term, however, balancing your time between work, family, and recreation makes life more fulfilling and less stressful.

REVIEW

True or False

Circle *T* if the statement is true or *F* if the statement is false.

T (F) 1. If a person is in the proper job, he or she will always be positive about that job.

(T) F 2. Low self-esteem can interfere with job performance.

T (F) 3. There is one right way to balance the demands of work and home.

(T) F 4. People who are different from each other can have good work relationships.

T (F) 5. Most people respond happily to unexpected changes in their life.

T (F) 6. The only way to learn something new is to return to school.

(T) F 7. A worker's initiative and interest may lessen after some time on the job.

T (F) 8. Having a sense of humor at work means making fun of coworkers.

(T) F 9. A poor diet and lack of exercise will sap your energy and make it harder to be productive.

(T) F 10. People often judge others by their appearance.

Check Your Understanding

1. List the three components of work attitude.
   <u>Attitude toward self, attitude toward work, and attitude toward the workplace.</u>

2. Why is it a good idea to examine your attitude regularly?
   <u>If you discover that your attitude is negative or that you are having a problem, you can take action to improve your attitude or solve the problem.</u>

3. List the ten strategies you can use to improve your attitude.
   <u>(1) Examine your attitude regularly, (2) balance work with personal life, (3) focus on the positive, (4) communicate, (5) turn unexpected changes into opportunity, (6) educate yourself, (7) maintain your interest, (8) maintain a sense of humor, (9) take care of your health, (10) dress for success.</u>

Topic 15

Succeeding in a New Job

DISCOVER

- techniques for making a smooth adjustment to a new job.
- why some jobs have a probation period for new workers.

Case:
The Newest Worker

Erica works on the cleaning crew at the hospital. Her dream is to work in foodservice. She has requested a transfer to the foodservice department, and her transfer comes through.

Erica arrives on her first day, eager to begin. She expects foodservice to be easy.

Her supervisor, Manuel, greets her and says, "Before you can start working, you must learn the basics of hospital foodservice. You will have three days of training. Then you will follow one of our staff on rounds to deliver and pick up trays."

Erica is shocked. It did not occur to her that she would have to learn anything. Erica is relieved that the training is not

Learn the written and unwritten rules of your workplace.

DISCUSS

1. What is your reaction to this case?

   Sample responses: Erica is too sensitive. Manuel should have explained the probation period better.

2. Do you think LaDonna was "mean"?

   Sample responses: Yes, she should have explained the probation period to Erica. No, LaDonna was behaving in a professional manner.

3. If you were in Erica's situation, what would you do?

   Sample responses: I would not have gotten depressed by LaDonna's behavior. I would have been glad that LaDonna and the others were such good teachers. I would have gotten angry with LaDonna.

too hard. After three days, she feels confident about her skills.

Now Erica is assigned to follow LaDonna on her rounds. LaDonna is polite and careful in explaining the job to Erica, but distant. At lunchtime, LaDonna leaves Erica to fend for herself.

Erica is beginning to feel depressed. She thinks, "Why is LaDonna so mean? Why doesn't she want to talk?" The maintenance crew was very jolly, laughing and joking all the time.

Erica follows other staff members on their rounds and learns from each of them. However, they are all distant, like LaDonna.

After a week, Erica helps serve and collect trays. After three months, Manuel calls Erica into his office. He says, "Congratulations. You have passed the three-month probation period. You are now officially a member of the foodservice department."

At the next staff meeting, Manuel announces Erica's new status. The group applauds enthusiastically. That day, LaDonna asks Erica to join her at lunch. Erica gladly accepts.

As LaDonna and Erica stand in the lunch line, Erica asks, "Why have you been so mean to me?" LaDonna says, "What do you mean?" "Well," says Erica, "you wouldn't chat with me while we were delivering trays; and before today, you ignored me at lunchtime."

LaDonna replies, "I'm sorry if I seemed mean. We don't like to chat while we are serving patients. It is so important to get the right tray of food to the right patient. If patients get the wrong food, they might get a bad reaction. In the worst case, a patient might get an allergic reaction and die! So we all try to focus only on our work while serving patients."

"And what about lunchtime?" asks Erica. LaDonna says, "So many people don't make it through the probation period. We don't like to get too friendly with someone who won't be staying. I'm so sorry that we seemed mean."

Erica feels much better now. She realizes that adjusting to her new job had many unexpected challenges. She now understands what LaDonna and the others were thinking.

ANALYZE

Starting a new job can be a stressful time. On one hand, it is exciting to meet new people and learn new skills. On the other hand, it is human nature to be uncomfortable in new situations and to worry about failing.

Good human relations skills can ease your entry into a new job. A positive attitude will help as you establish relationships with new coworkers.

Probation

It is normal to feel a little unsure of yourself in new situations. Think about the time when you started in a new school or joined a new club. As time went on and you observed the routine, you became more comfortable with your new situation.

Most workplaces have a probation period. **Probation** begins when you start a new position and usually lasts three months. During this period, you are not officially hired. Your supervisor trains you and observes how well you do. At the end of the probation, the final decision is made whether to keep you or let you go. Once you pass probation, you are officially a member of the team and are eligible for all benefits and responsibilities.

The hospital where Erica works has a three-month probation period. During this period, Erica received the basic foodservice training. Her supervisor, Manuel, was able to see how quickly she learned, what her work ethic was, and how she treated the patients.

Orientation and Training

Even if you have years of experience, you are likely to receive orientation for a new job, especially if you are new to the company. **Orientation** consists of presentations that describe your new company, its mission, and the basic rules. You are usually given the employee handbook. The **employee handbook** covers the detailed rules and regulations that employees must follow, such as what to do if you must miss a day. It also describes the employee benefits, such as health insurance and paid time off.

Many companies also provide training. Some companies provide training even if you are experienced in your area. For example, suppose you have a certificate in culinary arts. Each kitchen has its own way of doing things, so you are likely to receive training on the way your new employer wants things done.

Some companies are willing to hire people with potential and a good work ethic, then train them to do a specific job. The foodservice department where Erica works trains many people without experience. For these companies, the probation period is very important. They are willing to take the risk of hiring someone without experience. They need to be able to see whether the person can perform the job. If the person does not work out, the company needs an easy way to let the person go. Letting a person go during the probation period is less complicated than firing someone who has been hired.

Coworkers May Fear the Newest Worker

Anything that changes the **status quo** can be frightening. Even if a department desperately needs more workers, adding a new worker upsets the current situation. The existing workers have many questions. Is the new worker nice? Will he or she do a good job? Will he or she make mistakes and ruin the reputation of the company? Will the new worker be so good that he or she will get my job or the promotion I want?

When you are new on the job, you must treat all your coworkers with respect, no matter how they treat you. Some workplaces are very warm and friendly. Others are tense and fast-paced. If a company's ownership or management has recently changed, the workers may be nervous and afraid they will lose their jobs. In this situation, your new coworkers may treat you with suspicion.

However, all your new coworkers should treat you with respect. Be patient if they are distant for a while. Don't jump to the conclusion that they don't like you or that they are mean. They might just be afraid that you won't work out, the way LaDonna and the other foodservice workers felt about Erica. After they observe how you work, they may become friendlier.

Remember that you do not have to be friends with your coworkers, but you do need to have good working relationships. However, if anyone treats you in a way that harms or frightens you, you should let your supervisor know.

Few Pats on the Back

As a student, you may be accustomed to receiving frequent feedback on your work. Teachers give feedback orally and on written work and tests. Report cards are given at regular intervals, every six or nine weeks.

In most workplaces, feedback is rare. In many workplaces, workers get feedback only at the formal review, once a year. If the workplace is too busy, managers may skip the review.

A **performance review** is a formal evaluation of a worker's performance and productivity. The first review usually occurs at the end of the probationary period. After that, the review may occur on the anniversary of the worker's hire date. In some companies, everyone is reviewed at the same time each year, for example, the last week in March.

Most companies have a review form that the supervisor fills out for each worker. The supervisor then has a private meeting with each worker. At this meeting, the supervisor and worker discuss the review. Usually, the focus will be on areas that the worker needs to improve.

In the meantime, keep in mind that you might not be told the rules, procedures, and guidelines all at once. You might be caught by surprise when told that you have done or said the wrong thing. In many job situations, the only time you will receive a comment on your performance is when you make a mistake!

One of the best things you can do is learn how to take criticism in stride. Have a positive attitude toward constructive comments from supervisors or coworkers. You should thank the person for the helpful comments and vow to do better.

Learn the Rules

Workplaces have many rules, both written and unwritten. You will need to learn the rules as quickly as possible. During orientation, you will have received your employee handbook. Read it. These are the **written rules**. Flag the sections you may need to refer to in the future, such as what to do if you wake up ill and can't make it to work.

Most workplaces have **unwritten rules**. These are guidelines for behavior that everybody seems to know, even though they are not written down. You learn these rules by watching your coworkers. Do people stand in the hallway and chat, or do they only socialize in the lounge? Is it okay to be a little noisy, or does everyone speak in hushed whispers? Do people eat in the lunchroom or go out? If you are unsure about something, ask your supervisor or a friendly coworker.

DISCUSS

1. Do you think a probation period is a good idea?
   Sample responses: No, if you are hired then they have already evaluated your qualifications. Yes, there should be a period during which you can prove yourself.

2. Why would a company want to give you training even if you have already been trained?
   Each workplace has its own procedures, so each new worker needs training.

3. Why might existing workers fear a new worker?
   Sample response: The new worker might be better and get their promotions.

4. What do you think of the performance review system that most companies have?
   Sample responses: I don't like it; it makes me nervous. It's a good idea, like getting a report card at school.

APPLY

Case:
A Difficult Adjustment

You began your new job with high hopes and a positive attitude. You expected an initial adjustment period, but were not prepared for the lack of friendliness you encounter from your coworkers. You find that you don't have anything in common with them, and you are beginning to dislike them. You're not sure that you want to be a part of their group, even if they decide to let you in. You find yourself getting irritable and snapping at coworkers when they talk to you. Things are going downhill, and you are beginning to dread going to work.

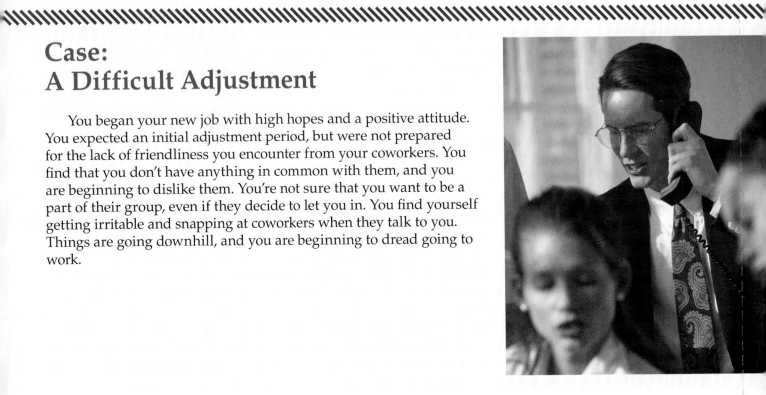

DISCUSS

1. List three options for dealing with your job situation.
   Option 1: __**Sample response: Tell your coworkers how you feel about them.**__

   Option 2: __**Sample response: Refuse to interact with your coworkers.**__

   Option 3: __**Sample response: Act in a friendly, professional manner toward all your coworkers,**__ __**even if you find it difficult, and focus on doing a good job.**__

2. List the option you would choose, and explain why you would choose it.
   __**Sample response: Option 3. If you act in a friendly, professional manner and focus on your job,**__ __**you will have the best chance of winning over your new coworkers. If you tell them what you**__ __**think or refuse to interact with them, you will make them angry and your situation will be more**__ __**difficult.**__

REVIEW

True or False

Circle *T* if the statement is true or *F* if the statement is false.

(T) F 1. Starting a new job is stressful for most people.

T (F) 2. Probation is a good time to mess around because a worker isn't really on staff yet.

(T) F 3. During orientation, a new worker learns about the company and its rules.

(T) F 4. The employee handbook covers the detailed rules and regulations that employees must follow.

(T) F 5. Adding a new worker can upset the existing workers, even if they desperately need the added help.

(T) F 6. A new worker should treat existing coworkers with respect, regardless of how they treat the new worker.

T (F) 7. Positive feedback is given freely in most organizations.

(T) F 8. It is a good idea to learn how to accept criticism.

(T) F 9. The unwritten rules of the workplace can be learned from observing the behavior of others.

(T) F 10. People can do a good job at work, even if they are not friends with their coworkers.

Check Your Understanding

1. Describe probation in the workplace.
   <u>Probation is the time after a person is hired when the supervisor observes how the new worker performs and decides whether he or she should be made a permanent worker.</u>

2. Why is it important to read the employee handbook?
   <u>The employee handbook will tell you what rules you have to follow and how to get the benefits that the company offers.</u>

3. How would you act if you were new on a job, and your coworkers were distant?
   <u>Sample response: I would treat everyone with respect and be friendly.</u>

4. What is a performance review?
   <u>A formal evaluation of a worker's work product.</u>

5. How can you learn the unwritten rules of the workplace?
   <u>Observe your coworkers or ask one of them if you have a question.</u>

Topic 16

Being a Reliable Employee

DISCOVER

- the negative impact of being absent or tardy on the job.
- ways to avoid being tardy.

Case:
Late Again

Blake rushes through the front door of the electronics store where he works. In his haste, he almost crashes into a customer on her way out. His boss, Richard, stands inside the door, arms crossed, looking very displeased.

"I'm really sorry, Rich." Blake tries to catch his breath. "It's just that my alarm didn't go off and…"

"Save the explanation. I'm not interested," Richard replies. "Did you recognize that customer you almost knocked over as you raced in?"

"I guess I didn't really notice. Oh, no!" Blake smacks his head. "I forgot! I was going to show Ms. Hunter the new stereo system we just got in stock."

Absenteeism and tardiness negatively affect your career.

"Well, she was here right on time," says Richard. "When I explained that you weren't here and the display model was still crated downstairs, she left. Didn't I ask you to assemble that system yesterday? What happened?"

"I was tied up with customers all morning, and then, well, I guess I left a little early."

"How early is a little early?" Richard asked. "Ten minutes? Two hours?"

"It's just that I had these tickets to the game, and with the traffic and all. I didn't leave too early." Even as he says it, Blake knows he is in big trouble this time.

"Blake, you know this equipment better than any other salesperson. I rely on you. When you're here, you are the best; but that's the problem. You are almost never here! I was looking over your attendance record. You are late almost half the time, and I can count on your missing work entirely at least once every two weeks. Do you realize that in the past three months, you've called in sick on six Mondays and twice on Friday?"

"I think my policies on absenteeism and tardiness are pretty liberal. I know my employees have lives outside of work, and I try to be lenient. However, you have abused my patience."

"Blake, I really hate to do this; but if you do not have 100% attendance and timely arrival for the next month, I will have to let you go."

DISCUSS

1. What is your reaction to this case?
   Sample responses: Richard is too strict. Richard is too lenient. Blake should know better and get to work on time.
2. What is Blake's attitude toward his job?
   Sample response: Blake seems not to care very much about his job.
3. What effect does Blake's behavior have on his job performance?
   Blake's poor attendance interferes with his ability to do a really good job.
4. Is Richard justified in criticizing Blake?
   Sample responses: No, Richard should make allowances for Blake because he is so good at his job. Yes, Blake should put his work attendance first, not his attendance at a sporting event.

ANALYZE

Imagine that you are a member of a sports team. It's the day of the big game. Your key player does not show up for the warm-up. In fact, he or she does not show up at all. How would this player's absence affect the game? How would it affect the morale of the rest of the team?

Two of the main problems that business owners face are absenteeism and tardiness. **Absenteeism** is being absent from work. **Tardiness** is arriving late to work. Most businesses have official policies for dealing with absenteeism and tardiness.

Lost Time Reduces Productivity

Think again about the sports team. What happens at a practice when one person shows up late? Everyone has to wait until the late person gets there. Valuable practice time is lost. The loss of practice time may turn into a loss at game time. If a player repeatedly misses practice, his or her skills will *not* improve. The other players will *not* learn how to work with the absent player. When players repeatedly miss practice, the team is weakened. This weakness is likely to cause losses at game time.

The same thing happens at work. Your supervisor and coworkers expect you to be there on time. Not only should you be on time, but you should also be ready to start working at your arrival time. If you are just stepping into the building at your 9 a.m. start time, it will be at least five minutes until you take off your coat, get to your desk, and take

out the project you are working on. If you stop in the employee lounge for coffee, it will be even longer. Meanwhile, you have lost this valuable work time and reduced your productivity.

If you have a job in which you serve customers, your lateness will result in poor customer service. Either no one will be there to serve customers, or your coworkers will have to cover for you. The result may be angry customers who decide to never return to your business.

One worker's tardiness or absenteeism causes stress for the other workers. They wonder why this one worker gets to arrive late. They may begin to resent having to cover for the late or absent worker.

Absenteeism Will Hurt Your Career

Absenteeism and tardiness can negatively affect your career, as Blake discovered. People judge you by your actions. Arriving late and missing days of work may be judged to be **unprofessional**. In other words, the tardy and absent worker is not meeting the high standards expected of excellent workers. Your coworkers and supervisors may feel that you are not serious about your career and your responsibilities.

Perhaps they are right. If you are often late for work or call in sick just to skip work, ask yourself why. It may be a sign that you don't like your job or your workplace. It may be a sign that you are irresponsible and need to grow up. If you can identify the cause of your problem, you can take steps to solve it. When the cause is solved, the symptom of tardiness is likely to disappear.

Official Policies for Time Off

Most businesses have official policies for time off. These policies are stated in the employee handbook. Be sure you get a copy of the employee handbook when you start a new job. Sometimes very small companies do not have written policies. In that case, ask what the policies are and write them down for future reference.

Certain types of workers are required by law to take a certain amount of time for lunch and breaks during the day. The amount of time and when you are to take it will be specified in the employee handbook. If you are not clear about the policy, ask your supervisor.

Even if not required by law, most businesses have specific policies on how long breaks and lunch times are and when they can be taken. Returning from lunch and breaks on time is as important as arriving at work on time.

Vacation Time

Most businesses realize that their workers need some time off for rest and relaxation. As a result, the businesses develop vacation time policies that balance the workers' need for vacation with the company's need to run efficiently. Usually, the number of paid days you get for vacation is related to the number of years that you have worked for the company. In addition, you usually have to submit an official request for the days you want to take off. Your supervisor usually has to agree that taking those specific days will not interfere with the department's productivity.

Emergencies Only

Most businesses also realize that illnesses and emergencies occur. They also have policies for handling these situations. If you wake up ill, most businesses require you to call your direct supervisor as soon as you realize that you are too ill to work. Many companies require a doctor's note if you are ill for more than three days. The company wants to make sure that you are well enough to return to work. If the illness is severe and will require a long recovery, most companies have special policies. In serious situations, it is important to be in communication with the company president or the head of human resources.

Businesses also realize that accidents and other types of emergencies occur. Weather can delay flights returning from your vacation site, and automobile accidents can keep you from getting to work. Again, most companies have policies for these situations. The most important first step is to call your supervisor as soon as you know you have a problem getting to work.

How to Avoid Tardiness

There are several strategies you can use to avoid tardiness.

- **Commit yourself to being at work on time, every day, after every break, and after lunch.** No excuses.
- **Allow enough time to get ready for work.** Don't try to do too many things in the morning. Focus on getting ready and getting out of the house.
- **Use 15 minutes before your actual start time as your goal arrival time.** This extra time allows you to hang up your coat, visit the restroom, get to your desk, and organize your work for the day.
- **Leave extra time for the commute to work, in case of traffic tie-ups.** If you know it takes 25 minutes to commute, leaving the house 26 minutes before your arrival time is not a good idea. Listen to the weather report the night before. If there is bad weather predicted, allow extra time in the morning. Listen to the traffic report in the morning. If there are traffic problems, cut your morning routine short to allow extra time to get to work.
- **If you drive to work, keep your car in good repair.** Dead batteries, empty gas tanks, and flat tires can often be avoided with regular maintenance.
- **When you plan to attend a special event, arrange for time off in advance.** If you have a good attendance record, your request will be looked upon favorably in almost every case.
- **Use days off to enjoy yourself, but don't return to work exhausted.** On your first day back to work, you want to wake up feeling fresh and ready to go, not exhausted and tempted to spend the day in bed.

DISCUSS

1. Name two things that don't get done because of Blake's tardiness.
   The display model of the stereo system does not get set up. A meeting with a customer, Ms. Hunter, could not take place.

2. What do you think of Blake's story concerning tickets to the game?
   Sample response: It is a poor excuse and not professional. It is a typical excuse but not a good one.

3. What effect do Blake's absenteeism and tardiness have on his coworkers?
   Sample responses: His coworkers may be angry with him because they have to do his work.

4. What effect could Blake's absenteeism and tardiness have on the success of the electronics shop?
   The shop could lose customers, like Ms. Hunter.

5. What advice would you give to Blake?
   Sample response: Shape up and get to work on time all the time.

APPLY

Case:
Everyone Else Is Late

You are a friendly and efficient employee. Customers and coworkers like you. You know that you are doing a good job and receive frequent compliments on your performance from customers. You have one big problem. Several of your coworkers are seldom on time. They arrive late—in the morning, after lunch, even returning from coffee breaks. You feel they are taking advantage of your high level of productivity. Your supervisor, however, doesn't seem to notice what the other workers are doing. You are tired of covering for them when they are not there.

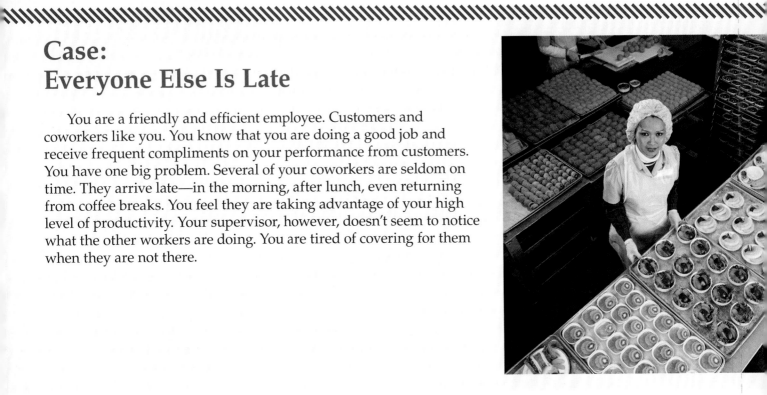

DISCUSS

1. List three options for dealing with your job situation.
    Option 1: __Sample response: Confront your coworkers and ask them to be on time.__

    Option 2: __Sample response: Complain to your boss about them.__

    Option 3: __Sample response: Focus on doing a good job yourself, and work on improving your work relationships with your coworkers.__

2. List the option you would choose, and explain why you would choose it.
    __Sample response: Option 3. Confronting your coworkers will just make them angry with you and will not improve the situation. If you complain about your coworkers to the boss, he or she might think you are not a team player. So the best thing to do is do the best job you can, and make your relationships with your coworkers as good as possible.__

REVIEW

True or False

Circle *T* if the statement is true or *F* if the statement is false.

T (F) 1. Employees who are five minutes late several days a week are a problem for businesses.

(T) F 2. Tardiness and absenteeism steal productive time from your employer.

(T) F 3. One worker's absence or tardiness affects other workers.

T (F) 4. People overlook absenteeism and tardiness if the worker is good at the job.

T (F) 5. All businesses have written guidelines on vacation time and tardiness.

T (F) 6. It is okay to take a sick day every now and then, even if you are not ill.

(T) F 7. It is unprofessional to often be late to work.

T (F) 8. Employers need to understand that a busy life and hectic weekend often leave workers exhausted and unable to get to work on time on Monday morning.

(T) F 9. When workers have good attendance records, employers are more likely to honor their requests for time off.

(T) F 10. It is as important to return to work on time after breaks as it is to arrive on time in the morning.

Check Your Understanding

1. How can absenteeism and tardiness interfere with the success of a business?
   When workers are late or absent, work does not get done or customers do not get served. When work does not get done, the company is less successful. When customers are not served, they may get angry and not return to the business.

2. How can absenteeism and tardiness interfere with a worker's success?
   If a worker is constantly late or tardy, the supervisor may view him or her as unreliable. The result could be that the worker does not get important assignments. In some cases, the worker could get fired.

3. List six ways you can avoid tardiness.
   Commit yourself to being on time. Allow enough time to get ready for work. Plan to arrive at work 15 minutes before your official arrival time. Leave enough time for the commute to work. If you drive, keep your car in good repair. Ask for time off in advance when you need to attend a special event. Be sure to get some rest during your days off, so that you return rested and able to get to work on time.

Topic 17

Career Plateaus

DISCOVER

- how to stay positive when you hit a plateau.
- strategies for coping with work plateaus.

Case: Changes in the Workplace

Riley has just marked his third year with CT. CT is a technology company that installs computer systems for small and large businesses. Riley started working at CT right after graduation from college. He has done very well and has high hopes for moving ahead in his career.

Riley learned the business quickly and is very good at his job. He has gotten good reviews, two pay raises, and more responsibility.

During his third year with CT, Riley was made project leader on a big contract. He developed a system for a small Internet company. The project went very well, and the client's

Stay positive during the ups and downs of career progress.

DISCUSS

1. What do you think of this case?
Sample responses: Poor Riley; he is stuck in a bad situation. Riley should stop complaining and do something to improve his situation.
2. What caused the change in Riley's situation?
The sale of the company.
3. What could Riley do to improve his situation?
Sample response: Take a course and improve his skills. Look for a job that gives him the opportunity to work in the areas in which he is interested.

online sales increased because of Riley's work. Riley got a large bonus. His boss, Yu-zhen, promised him more chances to be project leader. "You are doing an excellent job," she said. "You could be promoted to project manager within a year." Riley appreciated the praise. "Nothing can stop me now," he thought.

Within a few months, though, the president of CT announced that the company was up for sale. A large firm bought CT, and things began to change. The large firm is most interested in CT's expertise in servicing already installed systems. The newly combined company will no longer work with online technology.

At first, Riley remained a productive member of the programming department. However, he became bored working with installed systems. He missed the excitement of developing new programs. His ability to create systems for new online technology is no longer what the company needs.

Although Riley received an annual raise, it was much less than before. Yu-zhen tells him to focus on managing

people. "Go back to college and get a master's in business administration. Now that you're part of a big company, that's how to get ahead," she says. However, Riley does not really want to manage people; he wants to work with new technology.

As time goes on, Riley becomes more and more discouraged. He can see his career is going nowhere. "It just isn't fair," he tells Yu-zhen. "I'm losing my chance to grow. I've used up three years of my life in this company and nobody cares."

Riley's disappointment and negative attitude become obvious to his coworkers and to Yu-zhen. It takes him days to do the amount of work he used to do in hours. He takes long lunches and browses the Internet looking for interesting Internet companies. The others in his department have to work harder to pick up the slack.

When one of Riley's coworkers suggests joining a class in advanced programming, Riley says, "What's the use?" This becomes Riley's standard reply to any suggestions to enhance his skills.

ANALYZE

Most people begin their careers full of high hopes and ambition. The desire to get ahead and excel in your career motivates you to do your best. Your attitude is positive and constructive. You feel successful when your efforts are rewarded with more responsibility, raises, and promotions. Setting goals and working to achieve them increases your chances for career success.

When things are going well, it's natural to assume that the trend will continue. If you begin climbing the ladder of success, you may expect that your progress will be steady. If the situation changes, you might be thrown off course. Coping with the ups and downs of a career can be a challenge. Finding ways to stay focused and positive are essential to your career success.

Plateaus Are Normal

In the real world, progress toward your career goal may be slowed by **plateau** periods. In geography, a plateau is a flat area of land that is higher than the surrounding land.

During a **career plateau**, advancement stops. You stay at the same level in your job. Plateaus can last from several months to several years. Most people experience one or more plateau periods while pursuing their career goals.

There can be many reasons for a career plateau. If you are doing your job well and your career seems to be on track, the plateau is probably due to outside forces. You may be in a company where there are few openings in positions above yours. You may have to wait for someone to retire before you are promoted. Riley reached a career plateau when his company was sold. When a company changes structure or direction, workers' career goals are often affected.

Keep in mind that many people reach a certain level in their careers and are very happy. They do not wish to rise any further. They have reached their career goals. What might seem like a plateau to someone else is the top of the mountain for them.

Stay Positive

Keeping a positive attitude during a career plateau is essential to career advancement. It is easy to have a positive attitude when life is going your way. If you can maintain that positive attitude in a frustrating situation, your efforts will be noticed and appreciated by coworkers and supervisors.

How did Riley react to the frustration of his career plans? His attitude became negative and destructive. His productivity fell. His coworkers may eventually resent having to pick up the slack.

His boss will also notice the fall in his productivity and his change in attitude. She will no longer see him as having leadership qualities, and his chances for advancement will fall.

The key to weathering a plateau is to keep positive. The following strategies can help.

Talk with Your Boss

Even if there is no way to change the immediate situation, talk with your boss about your career goals. You may receive reassurance that the plateau will be short; you may not. In either case, your desire to advance will be on record. Don't damage your future the way Riley did. He complained about being treated unfairly. He let his productivity fall. He dismissed his supervisor's constructive suggestions. Riley let his anger turn him into a different worker. He has damaged his chances of being promoted.

Continue Your Education

A job that is not making full use of your abilities leaves you with more energy. Use the energy to polish your skills or learn new ones. Riley was shortsighted in not thinking about furthering his education. Do not make the same mistake. Getting training to improve your skills or learning a new skill may help you get out of a plateau period.

Keep a High Profile

Do *not* withdraw because you are unhappy. Speak up at meetings. Offer to train a new employee. Join in company activities such as the softball team or a fund-raising event. Serve on the planning committee for the annual holiday party. Write an article for the employee newsletter. Being active in these ways will bring you to the attention of upper management.

Accept Challenges

Do *not* turn down new assignments. Don't get stuck doing only what you like or what you feel you do best. There may be several ways to reach your career goal. A path that leads from one job to another is called a **career track**. The best career track for getting ahead may not be the one you chose. If another career track presents itself, seriously consider pursuing it. You might find that you like it better than expected.

Consider Leaving the Company

Consider all your options within the company before deciding to look outside for a new job with a new company. It can be hard to leave a company where you have been for a while. However, a career plateau may be a good time to consider moving on. For Riley, his current company is not the company he joined three years ago. The focus of CT's business changed with the sale of the company. Riley should consider looking for a job with a company that works with Internet companies.

When you decide to leave a company, continue to do your very best until you actually leave. You may have to work with that company and its workers in the future.

DISCUSS

1. What mistakes did Riley make?
   He let his attitude become negative. He did not analyze his situation and develop a plan to get what he wants.

2. What caused the change in Riley's attitude?
   Riley's change in attitude resulted from his own negative interpretation of events.

3. Describe how Riley could have responded in a more positive way.
   Sample response: He could have been grateful that he did not lose his job.

4. What might happen to Riley if he does not change his attitude?
   Sample response: He might get fired.

5. What advice would you give to Riley?
   Sample response: Improve your performance at work and look for a job more suited to your goals.

APPLY

Case:
Stuck on a Plateau

You have been working at your job for two years. The first year you received a raise and a promise of more responsibility if you kept up the good work. Now another year has gone by, and you are unhappy with your progress. You have not received a raise, and there has been no talk of promotion. When you ask about taking a training course to learn new skills, you are told there is not enough money in the budget this year. You have been a solid performer and have proven your loyalty to the company. Now you are beginning to question why you are not making the progress you had expected.

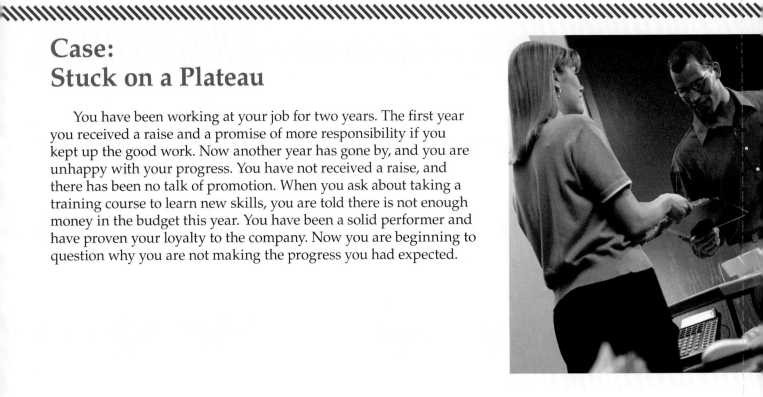

DISCUSS

1. List three options for dealing with your job situation.

   Option 1: __Sample response: Slack off; no one notices when you do a good job.__

   Option 2: __Sample response: Look for another job.__

   Option 3: __Sample response: Accept that you have reached a plateau and look for ways to keep your morale up and your visibility high.__

2. List the option you would choose, and explain why you would choose it.
   __Sample response: Option 3. Slacking off is always a bad idea. You don't want to look for a new job until you know there is absolutely no chance of advancement at your current company. So you accept the current plateau, keep your visibility high, and explore opportunities at this company.__

REVIEW

True or False

Circle *T* if the statement is true or *F* if the statement is false.

(T) F 1. Setting goals and striving to achieve them increases a person's chance for success.

T (F) 2. Highly productive employees almost never hit plateaus as they advance.

T (F) 3. Most workers reach their career goals without experiencing plateau periods.

T (F) 4. Plateau periods are most often caused by an individual's action or inaction.

T (F) 5. Maintaining a positive attitude during a plateau is almost impossible, and employers and coworkers understand this.

(T) F 6. What seems like a plateau to some people is the top of the mountain to others.

(T) F 7. When a worker hits a plateau, he or she should discuss it with the supervisor.

T (F) 8. Plateau periods are the perfect time to relax and take it easy at work.

T (F) 9. There is no good reason to volunteer for new assignments if the reasons for the plateau are beyond your control.

T (F) 10. When you reach a plateau, it's usually best to start looking for a new job right away.

Check Your Understanding

1. Why is maintaining a positive attitude during a plateau period important?
   It is important to maintain a positive attitude because if your attitude becomes negative and your productivity falls, you may ruin your chance for future career success.

2. What actions by a worker might cause a career plateau?
   Sample response: If the worker is not improving in his or her skills, the current job might be the highest one he or she can handle.

3. What are some outside forces that might cause a career plateau?
   There may be no open positions above you, the economic situation may be bad in the industry, or the company may have been sold and have new owners.

4. List five suggestions for how to stay positive during a career plateau.
   Talk with your boss. Continue your education. Keep a high profile. Accept challenges. Consider leaving the company.

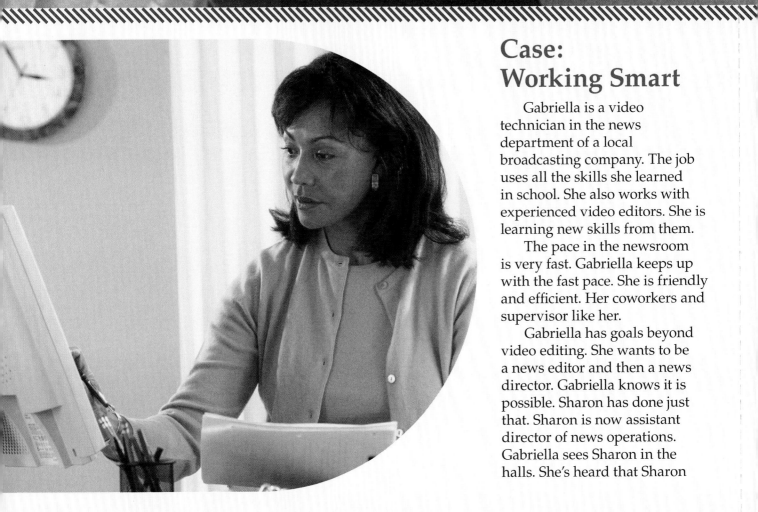

Topic 18

Planning Your Career Goals

DISCOVER

- how to set goals to help you advance in your career.
- how to work smart to improve your chances of promotion.

Case: Working Smart

Gabriella is a video technician in the news department of a local broadcasting company. The job uses all the skills she learned in school. She also works with experienced video editors. She is learning new skills from them.

The pace in the newsroom is very fast. Gabriella keeps up with the fast pace. She is friendly and efficient. Her coworkers and supervisor like her.

Gabriella has goals beyond video editing. She wants to be a news editor and then a news director. Gabriella knows it is possible. Sharon has done just that. Sharon is now assistant director of news operations. Gabriella sees Sharon in the halls. She's heard that Sharon

Choose your goal, then develop a plan to reach it.

DISCUSS

1. What is Gabriella's attitude toward her job?
   Gabriella has a constructive attitude toward her job. She goes above and beyond what is expected of her.

2. What is Gabriella's goal?
   To become a news director.

3. What does Gabriella do to reach her goal?
   She keeps up with the latest video-processing techniques, volunteers for difficult jobs, organizes her files, learns about other departments and the names of the department heads, and watches all the station's programs.

4. Do you think Gabriella will reach her goal?
   Yes

started in the video-editing room, but quickly moved on. "I want to be like her," Gabriella thinks.

The video-editing department is used by several shows at the station. Each show likes to have its work done in a certain way. Gabriella strives to make her work flawless. She keeps up with all the latest video-processing techniques. She volunteers to do difficult jobs that others do not want. She organizes her files of footage and labels them. This way, when a request is made, she can easily access the file. When footage from a previous broadcast is needed, Gabriella can find it quickly. The department head, Greg, notices what a timesaver her filing system is. He then asks Gabriella to set up a system for the whole department.

Because of her excellent work and creativity, Gabriella is given more-demanding jobs. She enjoys the challenges. Gabriella also works on learning about other departments in the company. She learns the names of the department heads and directors. She watches all the station's programs. She greets directors and producers by name and mentions their shows.

One day there is a breaking story of an out-of-control fire. Gabriella is assigned to help Sharon's team. They work overtime to prepare footage for the breaking story and news special. Sharon has an opportunity to watch Gabriella at work. She is impressed. Gabriella never complains or seems tired, even though they work late into the night. She pitches in and does whatever is needed. Gabriella is not afraid to speak up. She offers suggestions and ideas without being pushy. She is able to explain herself clearly and thoughtfully. Gabriella reminds Sharon of herself ten years ago.

When a job for a newsroom video supervisor opens, Sharon recommends Gabriella. After posting the job and interviewing several candidates, the director decides that Gabriella is the most qualified. When Gabriella is offered the job, she happily accepts.

ANALYZE

For some people, their work goal is to find the right job. Once they have found the right job, they are happy and productive. Their goal is to stay in their jobs and be the best they can be.

Others have the **ambition** to move onward and upward. Ambitious people want new challenges and responsibilities. Generally, the rewards are higher status and higher pay. The challenges may include difficult situations, harder work, and more stress. For some people, the rewards are worth the challenges. For those who want to move up in their companies, there are certain steps you can take to help you achieve your goals.

Be Clear About Your Goal

When you are in a job and know you want to advance, identify the specific job you want. Gabriella enjoyed her job as a video editor. As she became more familiar with the company, she identified her long-term goal: to become news director. Once she identified this specific goal, she could start taking steps to reach it.

If you are having trouble determining your goal, talk with your supervisor or human resources director. Many corporations provide support for people who want to climb the corporate ladder.

Identify Realistic Steps

Gabriella identified the first step on her path to news director.

She needed to be promoted to supervisor in the video-editing department. To put herself in a position for promotion, Gabriella needed to demonstrate several things: her technical and creative skills, her initiative, and her strong work ethic. She demonstrated her skills by keeping up with the fast pace of her job. She worked hard to turn in "flawless" work. She showed initiative by developing a way to organize files that impressed the department head. Because Gabriella works hard and works smart, she is given more-demanding jobs.

Gabriella also looked for a **role model** in the corporation. She has heard about and observed Sharon. Sharon is a woman who has reached her goals in the corporation. Gabriella learns about Sharon's career path, and determines to take the same steps.

In a corporation, it is also important to be friendly with everyone, but avoid getting too close to anyone. She keeps her relationships positive and business-like. She does not gossip or spend time socializing. She focuses on work. She also learns the names of other department heads and watches their shows. In this way, when she meets the department heads, she can talk knowledgeably about their programs.

Good job skills combined with good human relations skills are your ticket to success. A constructive attitude is important to your relationships with coworkers and supervisors. It is also an important element in career advancement. Gabriella would not have developed a reputation as an outstanding worker if she had only focused on her job skills. It was the

combination of good job and human relations skills, a constructive work attitude, and the influence of a role model that assured her success.

Do a Little Extra

Take every opportunity to show initiative. Volunteer for challenging tasks. Take initiative to do something to improve your department. Gabriella took it upon herself to reorganize the filing system for her video footage. The department head noticed that her new system made it so much easier to find footage. He asked her to share her system with the department. By sharing it with the department, she helped her coworkers become more productive. She earned their respect and that of her supervisor. At the same time, she increased her visibility and drew positive attention to herself and her skills.

Know Your Company

Learn as much as you can about your company. Know the products or services it offers and what each department does. Learn how your company is structured. Who are the department heads? Who does the hiring, firing, and promoting? Are people usually promoted from within the company or brought in from outside when an opening develops? Your chances to advance are greatest in a company that promotes from within.

Know Your Field

Keep up with the latest developments in your field. Read trade journals and magazines. Keep up with the latest news in the business section of your local newspapers. We live in a society where change takes place rapidly. Keeping up with trends, influential people, and events in your field gives you food for conversation with people on the job. Being aware of developments in your field is one way to let people know that you are interested in moving up.

Join the **professional organization** in your field and be active. Professional organizations often provide excellent trade journals and continuing education opportunities. In addition to the educational value, their meetings are good places to meet people and **network**.

Be Open to Opportunities

Be receptive to changes and opportunities. Gabriella was lucky to get an offer in the news department, where she wanted to go. What if she had been offered the video supervisor job in a different department? She would have been wise to take it. Opportunities don't always come exactly where or when you want them. When there is an opportunity for you to be promoted into a job that will help you grow and learn new skills, don't be afraid to take a chance. Look for opportunities to prove your ability.

Show Your Ambition

Let people around you see your desire to succeed. You do not have to be pushy or brag. Just show others by your actions that you have ambition. If your goal is a management position, prepare now. Take courses in

management and employee relations. Dress like a manager. Volunteer to lead projects. Offer to head a committee to solve a problem or develop a new procedure. Be willing to take the jobs that no one else wants. Become involved in your company's charitable efforts and special events. You may learn the most from the difficult projects.

Keep Your Attitude Positive

As you achieve your goals, do not leave your positive attitude behind. Good human relations skills are important no matter how high you go in an organization. Often, the higher you go, the more important relationships become.

Conduct yourself so that when your promotion is announced, others will be happy for you. Don't ever indulge in putting others down to get ahead. This type of behavior will damage your reputation. If you feel it is necessary to behave this way, perhaps it is time to think again about your goals.

When you are promoted, do all you can to make the transition smooth. Leave your work in order. Volunteer to train the person who will be taking over your present job. If that is not possible, write a memo to your replacement to provide information about the job. Include your new phone number, and let your replacement and supervisor know that you will be happy to answer any questions they have.

DISCUSS

1. What role did Sharon play in Gabriella's career plans?
Sharon served as a role model.
2. What did Gabriella do to show her competence?
She volunteered for difficult jobs.
3. What did Gabriella do to show her initiative?
She did extra work, organized her files, got to know other departments, and kept up with her field.
4. What did Gabriella do to show her work ethic?
She put in overtime and worked hard without complaining.
5. What do you think Gabriella will say to her coworkers when her promotion is announced?
Sample response: I am so excited about this opportunity! I look forward to working with you so that we can do the best job ever.

APPLY

Case:
Promoted over Your Friends

You are the top producer in your department. Because you are happy to help your coworkers, your excellent record is not resented but respected. You look forward to going to work every day. You genuinely like the people you work with. You often socialize with them after work and on weekends. In fact, you consider two of your coworkers your best friends.

The day after your supervisor announces he is moving to another city, you are asked to be his replacement. Although this has been one of your career goals, you didn't think it would happen in this department. Your supervisor is very young and you figured he'd be around for years. Now you are worried—how can you ever be an authority figure to your friends?

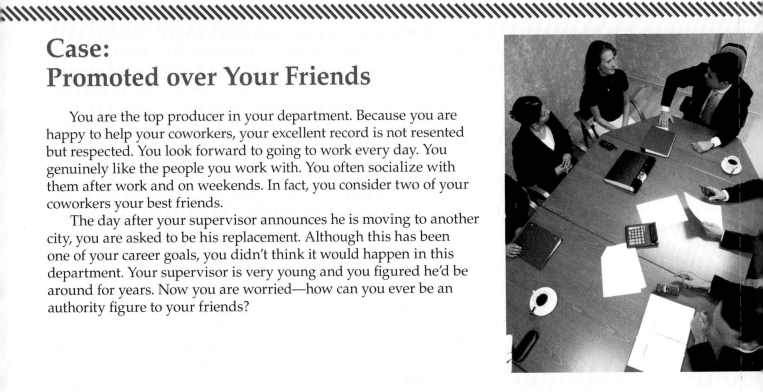

DISCUSS

1. List three options for dealing with your job situation.

   Option 1: __Sample response: Refuse the promotion.__

   Option 2: __Sample response: Discuss your concerns with your supervisor.__

   Option 3: __Sample response: Take a management training seminar.__

2. List the option you would choose, and explain why you would choose it.
   __Sample response: Option 2. Your supervisor probably recommended you for the promotion,__
   __so he must have a good idea of what your strengths are and can make some suggestions. You__
   __can also ask him about getting training. Option 1 is against your desire for a promotion.__

REVIEW

True or False

Circle *T* if the statement is true or *F* if the statement is false.

T **(F)** 1. Everyone has to have ambition for career success.

(T) F 2. The first step in career advancement is to define the goals.

T **(F)** 3. Goals that require numerous steps to achieve are not worth the effort.

T **(F)** 4. Excellent technical skills are all that is needed to reach career goals.

T **(F)** 5. It is okay to step on others to get ahead.

(T) F 6. Sharing good ideas that increase group productivity is a good way to show initiative.

T **(F)** 7. To get ahead, focus only on your department.

T **(F)** 8. Professional association meetings are a waste of time.

(T) F 9. Good human relations skills are important for career advancement.

(T) F 10. When people are promoted, they should volunteer to train their replacements.

Check Your Understanding

1. Do you have to be ambitious to achieve work success?
   It is not necessary to be ambitious to achieve work success. Many people are happy doing their best in one job.

2. List eight general steps that will help you achieve career success.
   Be clear about your goal. Identify realistic steps. Do a little extra. Know your company. Know your field. Be open to opportunities. Show your ambition. Keep your attitude positive.

3. How can a worker determine the best way to advance?
   Observe the people around you, learn about the structure of your company, and discuss career advancement with your supervisor or human resources director.

Part 4
Dealing with Problems on the Job

Topic 19

Learning from Mistakes

DISCOVER

- the positive side of making mistakes.
- strategies to use for dealing with mistakes.

Case:
Budget Blues

Business at the catalog company is booming. Anil started working in the shipping department when he was in high school. Back then, the company had only five employees. When Anil graduated, he began working there full-time.

Today, there are 20 full-time workers in the shipping department alone, and Anil is the assistant manager. The shipping manager, Hannah, admires his hard work and enthusiasm.

With Hannah's encouragement, Anil is attending college at night, majoring in business administration. Anil owes Hannah a lot. She has helped him move ahead in the company and has given him chances to try new things. When Anil was hesitant, Hannah

124

Copyright by Goodheart-Willcox Co., Inc.

Mistakes help you grow and can lead to success.

DISCUSS

1. What do you think about the way Hannah responded to Anil's mistake?
   Sample responses: Hannah had a right to be upset because the report was important to the department and her career.

2. What do you think about the way Anil responded when Hannah pointed out his mistake?
   Sample response: He responded in a responsible manner because he offered to correct his mistake.

3. What do you think is the best way to respond when you find out that you have made a mistake?
   Sample responses: Hide the mistake and hope no one will find it. Admit the mistake and correct it right away.

pushed him. "Test yourself, Anil," she always says. "I have confidence in you. You just need confidence in yourself."

Anil hates to make a mistake; but he does make some. Hannah never yells at him, even when he mailed a shipment to Portland, Maine, instead of Portland, Oregon. Her attitude is that mistakes happen. She is satisfied as long as you do your best, take steps to prevent mistakes, and correct those that happen. Her attitude makes it easier for Anil to admit when he is wrong. Overcoming his fear of failure has helped him gain the confidence to take on new assignments.

One Monday afternoon, Hannah calls Anil to her office and tells him that she is swamped with work. She must report on the cost of the expansion for the Friday meeting. "I've already calculated the staffing needs," she tells him, "but I need to prepare budgets for the cost of running your department, and I have to be in Texas tomorrow for that conference. I wish I could send you to Texas to speak in my place."

"Thanks for the vote of confidence, but I certainly don't have enough experience to speak in your place. However, I can finish the report for you. I know I can do it."

"Anil, this time I'm not so sure. You've never done budgets before. The decision to expand will be made at Friday's meeting, based on my report. However, I have no choice. You've done well in other areas. Give it your best."

Anil begins the report Tuesday morning. He works steadily, and the budget is on Hannah's desk by Wednesday evening.

Thursday morning, Hannah calls Anil to her office. Expecting a pat on the back, Anil is amazed to hear her say, "I'm afraid the figures you used to estimate mailing costs are outdated. You didn't factor in the postage increases."

Anil feels dizzy. "What was I thinking? I'd like the chance to correct my mistake."

"Well, it's a good thing you got this done a day early," Hannah said. "This mistake would have made management lose all confidence in me. I know it was just an oversight. The rest of the report looks excellent. Have the revised figures on my desk this afternoon."

ANALYZE

Everyone makes mistakes. The more you do, the more opportunities you have to make mistakes. The only people who make *no* mistakes are those who do nothing. However, they are making a major mistake by doing nothing.

Admit It

It may seem like a bad idea to admit a mistake. Won't people think less of you? However, once you make a mistake, it is better to admit it quickly, correct it if possible, and put it behind you. Don't make excuses for your mistakes. Fiorello LaGuardia was one of the most popular and effective mayors of New York City. He once said, "When I make a mistake, it's a beaut!" The voters liked him for his honesty.

In addition, history has shown that covering up a mistake can lead to more problems than the original mistake itself. The Watergate scandal is one of the most famous examples.

Do Not Make Excuses

Anil made a mistake that, if not caught, could have been costly. To his credit, he admitted it immediately. He did not make excuses or attempt to blame a third party. His quick apology and offer to correct his error confirmed Hannah's confidence in him. Taking these actions will also restore his confidence in himself. His self-confidence was shaken, but correcting his error promptly will help restore his confidence.

Do Not Fear Making Mistakes

Fear of making mistakes can be destructive. This fear can paralyze you and prevent you from taking any action. If you never try anything new because you fear you may make a mistake, you limit your opportunities for growth. Hannah took a chance on Anil; Anil took a chance on himself.

The outcome was that Anil stretched his abilities and accomplished something he had never tried before. Because of his ability and willingness to fix his mistake, Hannah is more likely to offer Anil new assignments. He will continue advancing in his career.

If you are a **perfectionist**, you are someone who dreads making a mistake. Fear of making a mistake can cause you to pass up opportunities that could advance your career. The worst mistake you can make is to refuse an opportunity because you fear failure.

Realize that it is not possible to do a perfect job all the time. Always do the best you can, but be realistic. Don't avoid new challenges out of fear of making a mistake. Remind yourself that most mistakes can be corrected. Use mistakes as a learning opportunity.

Learn from Mistakes

The ability to learn from mistakes can mark the difference between success and failure. If you allow yourself to quit every time you make a mistake, you will most likely fail to reach your goals. The only people who never make mistakes are those who never try anything new. View your mistakes as opportunities to learn and improve. Then you will most likely reach your goals.

Look at failure as a stepping-stone to success. Many of today's most successful entrepreneurs were unsuccessful in their first, second, third, or even fourth attempts at building a business. Rather than let these failures get them down, they learned from their mistakes. They took the knowledge they gained from failing and used it to achieve success. Follow the wise words of this famous saying, "If at first you don't succeed, try, try again."

DISCUSS

1. Why do you think Anil made the mistake in the report?
   Sample response: It is easy to forget that there will be a postage increase.

2. Did Hannah make a mistake in trusting Anil to do the report correctly?
   Sample responses: Yes, it was her responsibility, so she should have done it herself. No, she gave Anil the opportunity, and he did a pretty good job.

3. What do you think Anil learned from this mistake?
   Sample response: He should always anticipate cost increases when doing a budget.

4. What effect do you think this mistake will have on Anil's relationship with Hannah?
   Sample responses: Negative, Hannah will trust Anil less. Positive, Hannah was pleased with his quick offer to fix his mistake.

5. What effect do you think this mistake will have on Anil's future?
   Sample responses: It will ruin his future, as Hannah has lost trust in him. It will improve his future, as Hannah knows he will never make that mistake again and the rest of the work was good.

APPLY

Case: Oops!

As you are leaving work on Friday evening, your supervisor's phone rings. Since she has already left, you answer from your desk. It is an important message from the firm's largest customer. A problem has come up and your supervisor needs to bring additional information to the Monday morning meeting. You write the information on your phone message pad and head home.

On Monday morning, you arrive at work bright and early. You get right to work on an important project. Suddenly, you look at your message pad. "Oh, no!" you say out loud. You forgot to give the message to your supervisor, and she is already on her way to the meeting.

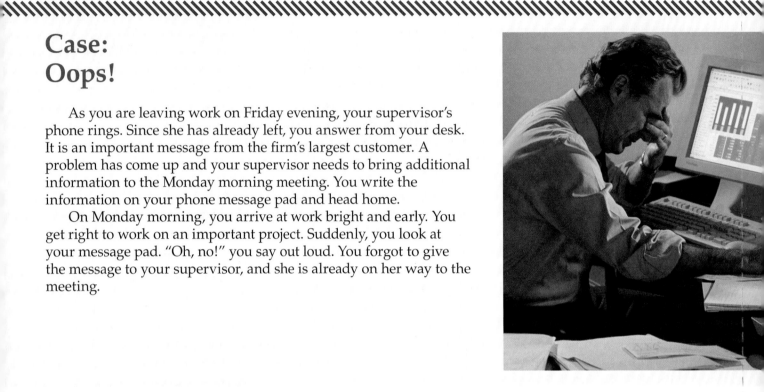

DISCUSS

1. List three options for dealing with your job situation.

    Option 1: **Sample response: Pretend that you never got the message.**

    Option 2: **Sample response: When the supervisor returns, admit your mistake and apologize.**

    Option 3: **Sample response: Collect the information that your supervisor needs, and take it to the meeting.**

2. List the option you would choose, and explain why you would choose it.
    Sample response: Option 1 involves lying and that is never a good idea. Option 2 is honest, but does not help the supervisor. Option 3 may be embarrassing, but at least you give your supervisor the opportunity to have all the information she needs.

REVIEW

True or False

Circle *T* if the statement is true or *F* if the statement is false.

T (F) 1. Efficient employees never make mistakes.

T (F) 2. Making mistakes will keep a person from advancing in his or her career.

T (F) 3. When the supervisor points out a mistake to a worker, that worker should immediately blame someone else.

(T) F 4. Fear of making mistakes can be more destructive than actually making a mistake.

(T) F 5. A perfectionist is a person who dreads making a mistake.

(T) F 6. The way a person reacts to mistakes can help or harm his or her career.

(T) F 7. When a worker makes a mistake, the best thing to do is admit it and work to fix it as soon as possible.

(T) F 8. A person with a constructive attitude sees mistakes as opportunities to improve.

T (F) 9. People with successful businesses became successful because they never made any mistakes.

(T) F 10. The only people who never make a mistake are people who never try anything new.

Check Your Understanding

1. Describe how making mistakes can help your career.
   <u>Sample response: If you learn from your mistakes, you will have more success in your career.</u>
   <u>Making mistakes often shows that you are stretching your abilities and accomplishments.</u>

2. Describe the advantages and disadvantages of being a perfectionist.
   <u>The advantage of being a perfectionist is that you try to do everything correctly and usually</u>
   <u>make very few mistakes. The disadvantage is that being a perfectionist could keep you from</u>
   <u>trying new things.</u>

3. Imagine that a coworker has made a mistake. What advice would you give him or her?
   <u>Sample response: Admit your mistake right away. Then take steps to correct the mistake as</u>
   <u>soon as possible. Work on ways to keep the mistake from happening again.</u>

Topic 20

Repairing Relationships

DISCOVER

- causes of damaged relationships.
- effective strategies to repair this damage.

Case: The Misunderstanding

Roberto breathes a sigh of relief as he finishes the last paragraph of the building proposal. It has taken a week of 12-hour days to collect information and write the proposal, but now it is done.

Roberto works for a local construction company. Samantha, the owner of the company, is his boss. With fewer new houses being built, the company needs to win this contract. If the company does not win this contract, there will be layoffs.

This is the first proposal Roberto has written. Writing proposals is an important responsibility in a construction company, and Roberto has

Act promptly to restore damaged relationships.

DISCUSS

1. What is your reaction to this case?
   Sample response: Harold jumped to conclusions. Roberto did a good job of trying to calm Harold down.

2. How would you describe Harold's behavior?
   Sample response: Jealous, angry, and unprofessional.

3. How would you describe Roberto's behavior?
   Sample response: Reasonable, calm, respectful and professional.

4. What do you think Samantha could have done to prevent the conflict between Harold and Roberto?
   Sample response: Samantha could have told Harold that she was giving the proposal to Roberto, and explained why.

let Samantha know that he wants to write them. Being chosen to prepare such an important document was a sign of Samantha's confidence in him. Besides, Harold, who writes most of the proposals, was tied up with problems at the Main Street site. Roberto proudly places the proposal on Samantha's desk.

The next day, Roberto heads outside for lunch. It looks like everyone is picnicking outdoors on this beautiful, sunny day. He joins his coworkers, and they all seem happy to see him—all except Harold. Harold does not return his greeting or even look at Roberto. As lunch progresses, Roberto realizes that Harold is ignoring him.

This worries Roberto, and as the group returns to work, he calls out, "Hey, Harold, hold on." Harold turns and waits for Roberto to catch up.

"Are you mad at me?" Roberto asks. "I felt like you were ignoring me at lunch. Did I do something wrong?"

"Don't act all innocent with me!" Harold replies angrily. "I came back early today to start writing the building proposal and discovered you'd already

finished it. What's the big idea? Are you trying to steal my job?"

"Hey, slow down!" Roberto is surprised by Harold's anger. "I wasn't stealing anything from you. You said you would be tied up at the Main Street site. Sam didn't expect you to be back in the office at all this week. That proposal was a top priority and you know it."

"Well, you certainly didn't waste any time taking over," Harold countered.

"Of course, I was happy to get the assignment. After all, I've been helping you prepare proposals for months now. You've been a great teacher. Don't you think it's time for me to have a chance to show what I know? Don't you think I can handle it?" Roberto asks. "Believe me, Harold, I'm not trying to steal your job. You're Sam's right-hand man and we all know it."

"I'm not sure you're ready for such a big responsibility," Harold says. "But maybe you're right. I guess I should've talked to you first." It isn't exactly an apology, but Roberto offers his hand in truce. The two men shake hands and walk inside.

ANALYZE

You are bound to have some conflicts with people on the job. Whatever the cause, when conflicts occur, the best response is to try to clear the air. To do so, you need to try to understand the other person's reactions and feelings. When Roberto noticed Harold's cold response, he asked him about it. If Roberto had tried to ignore it, nothing would have been resolved.

Once he found out what was bothering Harold, he tried to soothe Harold's hurt feelings. Roberto could have taken a different approach. What if he had said, "What's the big deal? You weren't here to do the proposal, so Sam asked me to do it. If you don't like it, that's your problem." This response would have made matters worse instead of better.

A misunderstanding can damage a relationship in the workplace. When conflicts occur, it is not always easy to forgive and forget. Remember, though, that communication is the key to good human relations. If you don't try to talk things through, you are risking permanent damage. In the long run, repairing damaged relationships and soothing ruffled feathers may be more important to your future.

Causes of Damaged Relationships

There are many causes of human relations problems. Conflicts are normal, but they should be resolved promptly. The objective is to avoid permanent damage in relationships.

Problems often arise when behavior is misunderstood.

In some cases, an attempt at communication goes wrong. Your tone, your words, or your body language might be sending the wrong message. Lack of communication can also cause problems.

Competition among coworkers is a common cause of conflict. **Competition** occurs when two people are after the same thing. It might be a plum project. It could be a promotion. Sometimes it's as simple as trying to get the boss to notice them. When each seeks to show the boss that he or she can excel, the competition can lead to conflict.

Lack of **common courtesy** is another cause of damaged relationships. It might be as simple as forgetting to say "thank you" when someone helps you meet a deadline. Your seeming lack of gratitude can cause a problem.

Being late on projects and causing others to fall behind can create problems, too. Absenteeism and tardiness can also create problems. Coworkers may become resentful when they have to fill in for you too often.

Strategies to Avoid Relationship Problems

When you are part of a team, be aware of other team members' needs. Use this awareness to avoid conflict. Let your coworkers know that you care about their feelings. Make a practice of showing good manners.

Even when you know people well, don't take them for granted. Show interest and concern for your coworkers. Be willing to do extra work without complaining. These actions will create good

relationships with your coworkers. As a result, if conflicts arise, you will have an easier time working them out.

The Dangers of Not Acting

Harold misread Roberto's motives. He was afraid that Roberto was trying to steal his job. Can you imagine the relationship between Harold and Roberto if they had not talked? Several things can happen if you do *not* try to repair a damaged relationship.

You May Spend Too Much Time Thinking About the Problem

You may find yourself replaying the scene over and over in your mind. You start thinking about everything the person has ever said or done. You begin to see innocent behavior as slights or insults. Anger and hurt feelings are likely to continue and might even get worse.

Damaged Relationships Add Stress

Like a toothache, an unresolved problem is always there. It's on your mind, even when you'd rather be thinking of something else. Most jobs have some stressful aspects that can't be changed, such as long hours, a heavy workload, or complex job tasks. Being angry or having someone else angry with you is a distraction that adds to stress.

Damaged Relationships Can Affect Your Productivity

Dwelling on a problem uses time and energy. Your productivity will start to slip. Often, when conflicts between employees arise, supervisors don't know whom to fault. They are likely to spread the blame evenly. These types of problems are often labeled as **personality conflicts**. Even though the conflict starts over a work issue, the lack of a solution is viewed as a personality problem. If you become known as a person who is involved in such a conflict, it can affect your overall performance rating. Employers expect mature people to resolve conflict and not let it affect their work.

Damaged Relationships Can Negatively Impact Your Career

It is possible to become a victim of a conflict. Imagine what damage Harold could cause Roberto if he stays angry. In the future, Harold might dwell on mistakes Roberto makes. He can avoid sharing information Roberto needs to do a good job. He might suggest to Sam that Roberto is not ready for more responsibility.

The Value of Good Relationships

Roberto will learn much more if he has a good relationship with Harold. Harold has been a mentor to Roberto. If Harold continues to mentor Roberto, Roberto will continue to learn and grow in his career.

Roberto is not the only person who gains from a good relationship with Harold. Harold can also gain. Roberto helps Harold's career by doing a good job. Roberto is smart. He can offer fresh ideas and help Harold solve problems. Harold has fewer worries and can focus on his big

responsibilities. Working with Roberto, Harold can show his leadership ability to Sam.

When Roberto and Harold work together, they make a productive team. As individuals, neither of them is as strong as they are combined. When coworkers like and respect each other, both feel good. When two people are joined in a relationship that is good for both of them, it is a **mutually rewarding relationship**. Both people benefit from cooperation.

Act Promptly

Resolve to act promptly to restore damaged relationships. Even if you are not responsible for the misunderstanding, take the first steps to repair it. Roberto's quick action helped to resolve Harold's anger.

Permit others to repair relationships with you. Do not give in to hurt feelings or nurse minor conflicts into major problems. To his credit, Harold listened to Roberto and allowed the healing process to begin.

In your dealings with others, resolve not to leap to conclusions. Do not always look for a negative explanation for another's behavior. Remember—like you, your coworkers and your supervisor are only human. Advancement in your career may very well depend on your ability to repair damaged relationships.

DISCUSS

1. What human relations mistakes are illustrated in this case?
   Sample response: Misunderstanding, lack of communication, and competition among coworkers

2. Have Roberto and Harold repaired their relationship?
   Sample responses: No, Harold is still angry with Roberto; Roberto may still have to prove himself. Yes, Harold listened to Roberto, and they shook hands.

3. How do you think Roberto and Harold will interact after this conflict?
   Sample response: Harold will see that Roberto is really a help to him, they will work together on more projects, and Roberto will get more responsibility.

APPLY

Case:
Angry Words

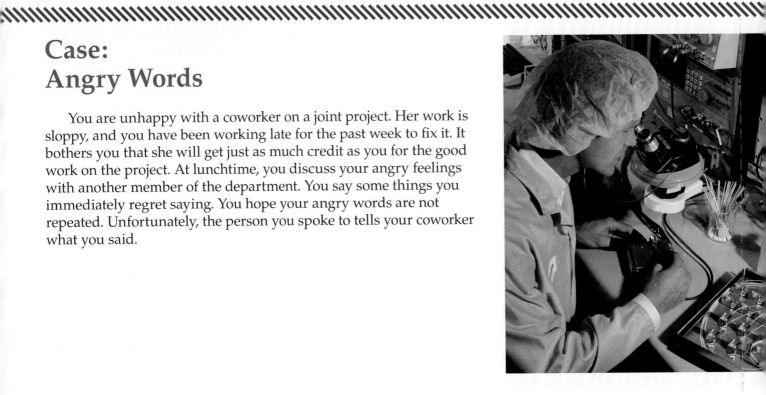

You are unhappy with a coworker on a joint project. Her work is sloppy, and you have been working late for the past week to fix it. It bothers you that she will get just as much credit as you for the good work on the project. At lunchtime, you discuss your angry feelings with another member of the department. You say some things you immediately regret saying. You hope your angry words are not repeated. Unfortunately, the person you spoke to tells your coworker what you said.

DISCUSS

1. List three options for dealing with your job situation.
   Option 1: __**Sample response: Ignore the whole situation.**__

   Option 2: __**Sample response: Angrily confront the person you confided in.**__

   Option 3: __**Sample response: Take responsibility for your actions, take steps to repair the relationship, and accept that you have learned a valuable lesson.**__

2. List the option you would choose, and explain why you would choose it.
   __**Sample response: Option 3. Ignoring the situation or confronting your lunch partner is likely to only make things worse. Accept that you have made a human relations mistake, vow never to make the same mistake, and repair the damage. Next time you get upset with a coworker, examine your reasons, then plan an appropriate solution.**__

REVIEW

True or False

Circle *T* if the statement is true or *F* if the statement is false.

(T) F   1. Misunderstandings and anger can permanently damage your relationships if allowed to go unrepaired.

T (F)   2. The time spent repairing damaged relationships could be better spent on improving productivity.

(T) F   3. Employees with constructive attitudes never end up with damaged relationships.

(T) F   4. Working with someone who is angry can add to a stressful situation at work.

(T) F   5. Damaged relationships can jeopardize a person's career.

T (F)   6. It always is the supervisor's responsibility to solve conflicts that arise among coworkers.

(T) F   7. The productivity of two people who work well together may be much higher than the sum of their individual efforts.

T (F)   8. The person who caused the disagreement should always make the first move to heal the relationship.

T (F)   9. A person is allowed to give in to hurt feelings and hold a grudge as long as he or she is not responsible for the misunderstanding.

(T) F   10. Career advancement may depend on a person's ability to repair damaged relationships.

Check Your Understanding

1. List seven causes of damaged relationships.
   <u>Misunderstandings, lack of communication, poor communication, competition, lack of</u>
   <u>common courtesy, absenteeism, and tardiness.</u>

2. List six strategies you can use to repair damaged relationships.
   <u>Act promptly, take the first step to repair the relationship even if you are not the cause of the</u>
   <u>problem, do not give in to hurt feelings, listen to the other person, do not leap to conclusions,</u>
   <u>and avoid looking for negative explanations for another's behavior.</u>

3. Why is it important to repair damaged relationships?
   <u>Sample response: Thinking about damaged relationships takes too much time and reduces</u>
   <u>productivity. Damaged relationships increase stress on the job and can interfere with career</u>
   <u>advancement.</u>

4. Describe the value of good relationships at work.
   <u>Sample response: Good relationships can lead to learning, job advancement, and increased</u>
   <u>productivity.</u>

Topic 21

Dealing with Criticism

DISCOVER

- why constructive criticism can help you succeed.
- how to give constructive criticism.

Case: The Troublemaker

Art class is Chen's favorite subject. Everyone admires his drawings. Chen believes that he has natural talent. He isn't very interested in learning theory or technique.

Chen's high school fine arts teacher believes that it is important to learn technique. Chen rejects his teacher's suggestions on ways to improve his drawings. Chen cannot handle criticism of his artwork. When his teacher makes suggestions, he feels personally attacked. He takes criticism as a sign that he has no talent.

Chen has his heart set on attending a famous art academy. The cost is very high, but Chen is convinced that he will be

Accept criticism and learn from it.

DISCUSS

1. What is your reaction to this case?
   Sample responses: Chen seems like a difficult person. I'm just like Chen. I know someone like Chen.

2. How would you describe Chen's attitude toward his job?
   Sample response: Chen has a negative attitude toward his job.

3. How would you describe the criticism that Chen received?
   Sample response: The criticism seemed reasonable and not that negative.

4. Why was Chen fired?
   Sample response: Chen was fired because he could not get along with others and work as a team member.

awarded a scholarship. He confidently sends his application and samples.

Chen is stunned when he is rejected. He is angered by the reasons he receives: "some talent, poor technique." "Those big city art snobs," he yells, "they can't even recognize talent when they see it!"

After failing to gain admission to art school, Chen decides to apply for a position as a drafting apprentice for an airplane manufacturer. He gets the job and starts the company's training program.

Chen attends a three-month training course. He is surprised that he likes drafting so much. He likes the detail work. In a way, it is like being an artist. He is drawing and doing something useful with his talent.

Chen trains with a veteran drafter for one year. He is not given much responsibility, but he is learning his trade. In this situation, Chen accepts criticism of his work. He feels that because he is an apprentice, he is supposed to be learning.

When his apprenticeship ends, Chen is assigned to the electrical department. Now he is given jobs to do on his own. When there is a problem with one of his drawings, the designers and engineers discuss it with him. Unfortunately, Chen's difficulty with accepting criticism returns. Because he is now a trained drafter, Chen feels that he knows how to do his job. He becomes upset whenever he has to make corrections to his work. He feels he is failing in his new job.

Chen begins to resent the engineers and designers. He feels that they think they're better than he is because they have more education. When one of them questions his placement of a wire, he sulks for the rest of the day.

Chen has a great deal of trouble working on a team with other drafters. When Chen's ideas are not used, he is personally insulted. Chen refuses to talk to some members of the department because they have changed his drawings. He is quickly earning a reputation as a troublesome member of the department.

After Chen has worked as a drafter for 18 months, his boss is forced to cut the staff. Although Chen has more talent than many of the others, Chen is let go.

ANALYZE

Everyone faces **criticism** at one time or another. Criticism might be fair or it might be unfair. It might come from a source you respect or from someone you don't trust. In the workplace, criticism is to be expected. Being able to accept criticism and to learn from it is an important human relations skill.

Being Criticized Can Hurt

Criticism hurts. When you do your best, you don't want to be told it's not good enough. Even when you know you are wrong, criticism can sting. Many people are not good at delivering criticism. It might be hard for them to sound constructive. At work, your supervisor might wait until review time and give you a long list of mistakes all at once.

To avoid the hurt from criticism, learn how to accept criticism as a part of life. Do *not* think of criticism as an evaluation of your whole being. One of Chen's mistakes is generalizing criticism of his art or work to his whole life. When his art teacher makes suggestions, Chen feels the statements mean he has no talent. When the designers and engineers make suggestions, Chen thinks he is failing in his new job.

A balanced view of yourself can help you handle criticism. Be willing to admit when you are wrong. Develop a "thick skin," and try not to be **defensive**. Being defensive means that you refuse to accept responsibility for your mistakes. Instead, you blame others or make excuses. A better response is to listen calmly to criticism and be willing to learn from it.

Here is another approach that is helpful on the job. Remember that your goal is to produce the best product for your customer. Suggestions and criticisms are

offered to improve the product for your customer. Therefore, you should not take criticisms at work personally.

Constructive Criticism Helps You Learn

Criticism can be a learning experience. **Constructive criticism** is criticism given to help you learn. Chen's art teacher offered him constructive criticism. He wanted to help Chen improve on his natural talent. Unfortunately, Chen's defensive attitude prevented him from benefiting from his teacher's feedback. He was unable to accept the constructive advice. Instead, Chen interpreted the criticism as a personal attack. Because Chen could not accept constructive criticism, his artwork did not improve and his application to art school was rejected.

Criticism intended to inflict hurt is **destructive criticism**. Its intention is to wound, not teach or help. Destructive criticism is often motivated by anger. Imagine how Chen would have felt if his teacher had said, "Whatever made you think you were an artist? Look at this dreadful drawing!"

Constructive criticism is not given in anger or as a criticism of you personally. Imagine that Chen's teacher criticized his work this way, "Chen, I like the subject matter you've chosen, and this drawing shows that you have talent. I see you're having a problem with the perspective. Why don't you review the techniques in Chapter 12 of the text?"

However, Chen never learned the difference between constructive and destructive criticism. He never learned to accept criticism and benefit from his mistakes. Ultimately, it cost him his job. Although he has good drafting ability, his destructive attitude toward criticism interfered with his relationships and progress at work.

When You Criticize Others

At some point, you may be in the position to give criticism. Perhaps you will be part of a team that is evaluating a project. Perhaps you will be promoted to supervisor. Do not give criticism when you are angry. Give yourself time to calm down and logically analyze the situation. Give yourself time to plan what you need to say.

When you give criticism, make it constructive. Do not attack the person. Criticize the work or idea by giving concrete, provable reasons for the problem. Then offer suggestions for solution. Imagine you are the person you must criticize. Give criticism the way you would like to receive it.

DISCUSS

1. What do you think is the cause of Chen's feelings about criticism?
   Sample responses: Chen may actually have low self-esteem. He may be a perfectionist and cannot handle being wrong.

2. Describe what might have happened if Chen had responded positively to the criticism from his art teacher.
   Sample response: Chen's work might have improved, and he might have gotten into art school.

3. Describe what might have happened if Chen had responded positively to the suggestions from the designers and engineers at his job.
   Sample response: Chen's work might have improved, and he would have gotten along better with his coworkers. He might not have gotten fired.

4. What advice would you give to Chen?
   Sample response: Find out what is bothering you and solve that problem, or you might never find a job you can keep.

APPLY

Case:
The New Supervisor

You have been promoted to supervisor. You feel able to handle your new duties. The only problem you are having is with one employee who is not performing well. Rather than doing the most important tasks, he does the easiest work and lets the rest sit. He is taking long lunch hours and making personal phone calls when he should be working. You need to discuss his job performance with him.

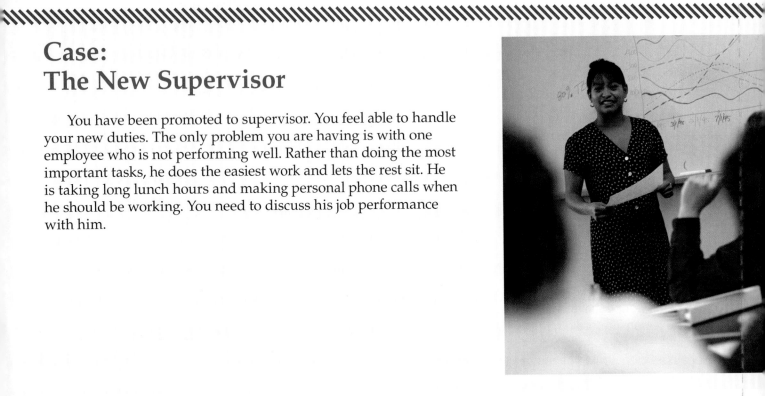

DISCUSS

1. List three options for dealing with your job situation.

   Option 1: **Sample response: Ignore the situation and assume that he will do better.**

   Option 2: **Sample response: Yell at him and tell him what a poor job he is doing.**

   Option 3: **Sample response: Ask him to meet with you to discuss his performance, and have him prepare his own performance evaluation.**

2. List the option you would choose, and explain why you would choose it.
   Sample response: Ignoring the situation or yelling at him will not solve the problem. By following Option 3 and having him do his own evaluation, you can get him started thinking about whether he is doing a good job. He might realize before you tell him that he has not been performing to expected standards.

REVIEW

True or False

Circle *T* if the statement is true or *F* if the statement is false.

(T) F   1. Criticism hurts.

T (F)   2. Workers with positive and constructive attitudes escape criticism.

(T) F   3. Constructive criticism is given to help workers learn and improve.

T (F)   4. All criticism is constructive.

T (F)   5. Destructive criticism, although painful, offers suggestions for improving a worker's performance.

(T) F   6. Criticism should never include a personal attack against another.

T (F)   7. Criticism given in anger is more effective.

(T) F   8. The failure to accept constructive criticism can interfere with productive relationships.

(T) F   9. The ability to learn from mistakes can lead to career success.

(T) F   10. The ability to give constructive criticism and avoid giving destructive criticism is an important supervisory skill.

Check Your Understanding

1. Describe constructive criticism.
   Constructive criticism consists of suggestions to help you do something better; it is designed to help you learn and improve.

2. Describe destructive criticism.
   Destructive criticism is designed to hurt someone and is often given in anger.

3. Why does criticism hurt?
   Sample response: Criticism hurts because it includes negative comments about something you have done and perhaps worked very hard at.

4. How can constructive criticism help you on your job?
   Sample response: Constructive criticism can show where you are making mistakes or where you need to learn more skills. When you correct the mistakes and learn more skills, you will be more successful at work.

5. Give three suggestions for how to give constructive criticism.
   Sample response: Give concrete reasons for the criticism. Offer solutions. Give criticism the way you would want to receive it.

Topic 22

Leaving a Job

DISCOVER

- how to decide when it's time to leave a job.
- ways to leave a job in a positive manner.
- what to do if you are fired.

Case: Ready to Move On?

Austin has worked at a local accounting firm for three years. He majored in accounting in college, and this is his first job. He was hired as a junior accountant. The owners, Jonathan and his wife, Jennifer, treat Austin very well. He feels a deep loyalty to them.

During his second year with the firm, Austin decided to take courses at night to become a certified public accountant (CPA).

While attending school, Austin received support and encouragement from Jonathan and Jennifer. "Work hard and you will succeed, Austin," they told him. "There is a good future for you here."

Analyze your reasons before you leave a job.

DISCUSS

1. What is Austin's attitude toward his job?
   Austin has a positive, constructive attitude toward his job.

2. How would you describe Jonathan and Jennifer as bosses?
   Sample response: Nice, professional, and supportive.

3. What do you think Austin should do? Why?
   Sample responses: Stay with his current company because his coworkers are so nice. Find a job with a national firm so he can be challenged and travel.

When Austin passed the CPA exam, his coworkers threw him a surprise party. Soon after, Jonathan and Jennifer promoted Austin to senior accountant. Now in his third year with the firm, he is again promoted. His new position is manager of the tax preparation unit. Austin is excited about managing.

Austin joined a professional association, the American Institute of Certified Public Accountants (AICPA). At the meetings, Austin meets people who work for large corporations and accounting firms. He starts thinking about what it would be like to work for a large company. He notices that people in big firms often travel and have more opportunities for advancement.

Austin doesn't want to leave just because his firm is not big enough. "Maybe," he thinks, "I can stay and help the firm grow."

He asks Jonathan and Jennifer about their future plans for the firm. He tells them how they could make it grow. The owners listen intently and praise his initiative. However, they like their firm the way it is. "Small businesses are key to the economic health of our community," says Jennifer. "When they succeed, we succeed. We are not interested in large, national accounts."

Jonathan tells Austin they understand his frustration, but adds, "You're young. Be patient, Austin. By the time someone retires in fifteen or twenty years, you'll be in a position to become a partner here."

Austin doesn't want to wait that long. He wants to make quicker progress. He needs more challenge and excitement in his work. He wants more money and responsibility.

Austin speaks to his friend, Fatima, who works for a national consulting firm. Fatima suggests that he talk with people who have jobs in national firms. She offers to introduce him to the senior tax advisor in her firm.

Austin meets with the tax advisor. He likes what he hears. Austin decides to start looking for a job in a national firm. He also decides to network with AICPA members who work for national firms.

ANALYZE

How long you stay in a job depends on many factors. You might like your first position and stay there, or you might move up the ladder. Deciding when it is time to move on is an important step. Leaving a job in a positive manner is equally important.

When Is the Right Time to Leave?

Whether to leave a job is a serious decision. Here are some clues that indicate that you should start thinking about leaving.

- You dread going to work.
- You have trouble getting to work on time.
- Your productivity is falling.
- You have gotten a negative performance review.
- You are bored.
- You want to move up the ladder, but there are no openings.

If you have any of the above feelings, it does *not* mean that you should automatically start looking for a new job. It *does* mean that you should find out the reason for your feelings and look for solutions at your current workplace.

Analyze Your Reasons

If you dread going to work because of people around you, try to resolve the problem. It is rarely a good idea to leave a job because of a personality conflict. Your supervisor or your human resources department may be able to help you resolve personality conflicts.

If the problem stems from a destructive attitude on your part, changing jobs almost never helps. Your negative attitude will travel with you. Find out the reasons for your negative attitude and work to correct it. You may need counseling.

Suppose you are having trouble getting to work, your productivity is falling, or you received a negative performance review. Ask yourself, "Am I having health, family, financial, or other outside problems?" Such problems could be causing your poor performance. If these problems are not solved, you are likely to take them with you to your next job. It might be better to stay at your current job, and get help to solve your problem. Many companies provide resources to help workers resolve problems.

If you are bored, consult your supervisor or human resources department. Perhaps you can get special training or be placed on a special project. There may be another job in the company that would be more challenging. Austin went back to school for his CPA. Soon after, he was promoted to senior accountant.

If you want to move up the ladder, discuss it with your supervisor or human resources department. You may discover opportunities that you did not know existed. If you discover that there is no way for you to advance, then consider looking for a new job.

Overcome Inertia

Changing jobs is not easy. Your current job is safe, comfortable, and familiar. In the workplace, **inertia** means a reluctance to make changes. Some people stay in jobs because of inertia or fear of the

unknown. They are happy enough, and see no reason to change. For some people, the safe decision may be the best decision. There is no shame in staying in a job where you are reasonably happy and reasonably productive. However, if you are very unhappy, then it might be worth the risk to make a change.

If Austin decides to stay because of a sense of gratitude, loyalty, or a desire for a familiar and comfortable job, it would most likely be a mistake. Eventually, his dissatisfaction and frustration might undermine his positive attitude toward his job. If that begins to happen and he still stays, his productivity might fall and his relationships with his coworkers may deteriorate.

In some careers, you are expected to make many job changes. Employers realize that you learn new things with each new job. If you are in one of these careers and want to advance, you will have to learn how to deal with the risk of changing jobs.

Leave in a Positive Way

Once you have made the decision to leave, stay positive. Keep your productivity level high even while job hunting. Your present employer is still your first priority.

Do *not* use any of your current employer's resources for your job hunt. Do not use time at work, the computer, company letterhead or envelopes, the phone, or mailing services. If you need time, take vacation time.

Do not **resign** your current job until you have a letter from your new employer stating when you will start. You would be in a difficult situation if the new job fell through after resigning from your current job.

When you have accepted another job, you must give notice. **Giving notice** means telling your supervisor that you intend to leave your job. The first step is to write a **letter of resignation**. Address the letter to your supervisor. In the letter, express appreciation for the time you spent with the company, express regrets at leaving, and give the date of your last day. Next, meet with your supervisor, tell him or her that you are leaving, and provide your letter of resignation. Offer to train your replacement or help in whatever way you can to make the transition easier for the company.

With your supervisor, coworkers, and human resources personnel, stay positive about your reasons for leaving. Resist the urge to make negative comments about your coworkers, supervisor, or the company. Do not make unfavorable comparisons between your present job and your new one. Leave on a positive note, and you will keep all your future options open. You may work with these coworkers in the future. Some day you may want to return to the company, or one of your current coworkers may move to your new company.

What to Do If You Are Fired

Sometimes, the choice to leave a job is not your own. You may be **fired**. There are two types of firing: for cause and due to circumstances beyond your control.

Being fired for cause means that you have done something that harms the company or you have not been performing up to standards. In most companies, using alcohol or illegal drugs at work, physically harming another employee, or stealing company property are grounds for immediate dismissal.

If you have not been performing well, most companies give you one or more chances to improve your performance. If you do not improve within a specific time period, you will be let go.

The other type of firing is due to circumstances beyond your control. Many companies hire employees with the understanding that employment can be terminated at any time and for no specific reason. This is called **at-will employment**. You or the employer has the right to terminate your employment at any time.

When a company is in financial trouble or is bought or sold, the result is often the firing of many people at the same time. When positions are cut, the term used is **layoff**. Another term for this is **reduction in force (rif)**.

If you are laid off or riffed, you may feel angry, sad, or depressed. These are typical responses. However, keep a positive attitude. Do not spoil a good work record with words spoken in anger. Do not say anything negative about the company or your coworkers. The company may call you back when conditions improve. Some day, you may work with the same people or the same company.

When you are notified that you will be laid off, understand all your negative emotions, but do your best to control them. Losing your job will be even more serious if you lose your positive attitude with it. Immediately update your résumé and start looking for a new job. Network and go to meetings of professional organizations.

DISCUSS

1. What did Austin do to improve his job situation? **He got his CPA, joined AICPA, and attended AICPA meetings.**
2. Why is Austin considering leaving his job? **He wants more money and responsibility.**
3. What did Austin do to explore new job possibilities? **He joined a professional organization, AICPA, and attended meetings. He discussed his career goals with a friend who works for a national firm.**
4. Did Fatima give good advice to Austin? Why or why not? **Yes, she listened to him, told him what she heard him saying, and introduced him to someone who could tell him more about the kind of work he is interested in.**
5. Describe how Austin should give notice. **Sample response: He should ask to meet with Jonathan and Jennifer. He should tell them how much he has enjoyed working for them and how much he has learned from them. However, he wants the challenge of a national firm, so that is why he is resigning to take a position at the new firm. He should also give them a letter of resignation.**

APPLY

Case:
Dealing with a Layoff

You are an employee who is highly valued by your manager. In your six months on the job, you have received excellent feedback. You love your job, have a good relationship with your coworkers, and plan to work in this company for a long time. Unfortunately, budget cutbacks cause a layoff. Although you are an ideal employee, you are also the newest person hired. Your company has a layoff policy based on seniority; that is, in time of layoffs, the newest workers are fired first. The worker who will be assuming your duties is not as capable as you are. You are angry and frustrated.

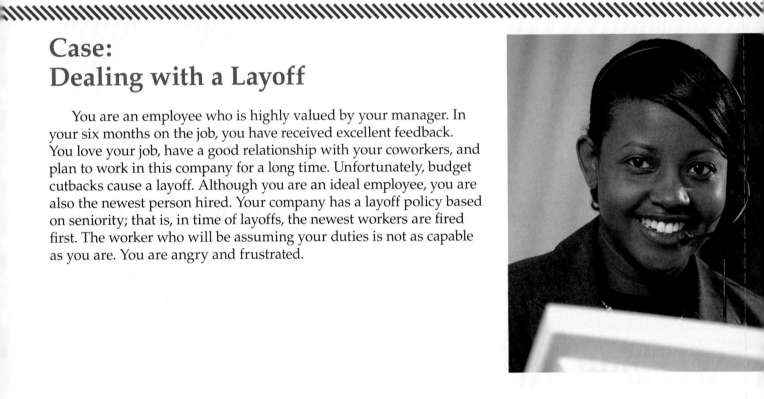

DISCUSS

1. List three options for dealing with your job situation.
   Option 1: __Sample response: Tell everyone how unhappy you are and how unfair the company__
   __is being.__

   Option 2: __Sample response: Quit before they fire you, and refuse to train the new person.__
   _____

   Option 3: __Sample response: Offer to train the new person and let everyone know how sorry__
   __you are to be leaving.__

2. List the option you would choose, and explain why you would choose it.
   __Sample response: With Options 1 and 2, you are burning your bridges and can never return__
   __there to work. Option 3 is the professional way to act and leaves everyone feeling good about__
   __you. The company is likely to invite you back if the situation improves.__

REVIEW

True or False

Circle *T* if the statement is true or *F* if the statement is false.

T (F) 1. People usually change jobs after two years.

(T) F 2. Some people stay at a job they do not like because of fear of the unknown.

T (F) 3. Loyalty to the worker's current employer is a good reason to stay at a job.

(T) F 4. Unhappiness is one clue that it may be time to look for a new job.

T (F) 5. When a person decides to look for a new job, he or she does not have to put any effort into the current job.

(T) F 6. If a person has a destructive attitude, it will usually follow him or her to a new job.

(T) F 7. When a worker has accepted a new job, he or she should write a letter of resignation to the supervisor.

T (F) 8. It is okay to say negative things about the company after accepting a new job.

(T) F 9. Many people become angry, sad, or depressed when they lose a job.

T (F) 10. It is okay to use the current employer's stationery and computer when applying for a new job.

Check Your Understanding

1. List six clues that you should consider when looking for a new job.
   <u>You dread going to work. You have trouble getting to work on time. Your productivity is falling. You received a negative performance review. You are bored. You want to move up the ladder, but there are no openings.</u>

2. If you experience one of the six clues, does that mean you should leave your job immediately? Explain your answer.
   <u>No, it means you should analyze your reasons for these feelings. Once you determine the cause, you can better decide what steps to take.</u>

3. Why should you *not* use your current employer's resources when you look for a new job?
   <u>Using company property for projects that are not part of your job tasks is stealing. Also, your coworkers or supervisor may hear your conversations or find drafts of your résumé.</u>

4. Describe a positive way to leave a job.
   <u>Sample response: Write a letter of resignation, meet with your supervisor to tell him or her that you are leaving, provide a resignation letter, and offer to train your replacement.</u>

Glossary

A–C

absenteeism. Missing a day of work. (16)

accepting responsibility. Being willing to answer for your actions and decisions. (11)

ageism. Prejudice based on age. (6)

aggressive behavior. Behavior that is hostile or threatening. (9)

ambition. Desire for rank, fame, or power. (18)

attitude. Belief or feeling that causes you to act in a certain way. (2)

at-will employment. Understanding that the company can let you go, or you can resign, at any time. (22)

bigot. Person who lacks tolerance for others; a prejudiced person. (6)

body language. Communication that uses gestures, facial expressions, and actions; another term for *nonverbal communication*. (1)

career plateau. Period of time when career advancement stops. (17)

career track. Path that leads from one job to the next higher job. (17)

common courtesy. Polite behavior and good etiquette, such as saying "please" and "thank you." (20)

communication. Sending messages from one person to another. (1, 12)

competition. Contest between two or more people to reach the same goal, such as a promotion. (20)

confidence. Feeling able to handle challenges. (8)

confidential information. Private information intended for selected individuals. (10)

conscientiousness. Quality of being committed to doing what is right and proper. (13)

consequence. Result. (11)

constructive attitude. Attitude that combines friendliness with taking action to get results. (7)

constructive criticism. Criticism given to help you learn. (21)

cooperation. Working together for the common good. (3)

coworker. Person who works with you. (4)

criticism. Finding fault; feedback, often negative. (21)

D–F

defensive. Refusing to accept responsibility and blaming others. (21)

dependability. Quality of doing what you say and following through on your promises. (13)

destructive criticism. Criticism intended to hurt. (21)

discrimination. Negative actions based on prejudice and targeted at individuals. (6)

dissatisfaction. The state of always being unhappy, always seeing the negative. (6)

employee handbook. Book that covers rules that employees must follow, such as what to do if you must miss a day; also describes employee benefits, such as health insurance and paid time off. (15)

favoritism. Special attention shown to someone in a group of people who are all supposed to be treated equally. (5)

fired. Let go from a position with a company. (22)

G–I

giving notice. Telling your supervisor that you intend to leave your job. (22)

goodwill. Positive feeling toward another person or business that occurs when that person or business does something nice for you. (7)

gossip. Rumors about the personal, private lives of people. (10)

hierarchy. Ranking people based on the level of their jobs. (4)

honesty. Quality of telling the truth and *not* stealing. (13)

human relations. Study of how people interact with each other. (1)

human relations skills. Skills used to make interactions with people as positive as possible. (1)

impartial. Not taking sides. (4)

inertia. Reluctance to make changes. (22)

initiative. Quality of self-motivation; the ability to get the job done on your own. (13)

integrity. Good character; being dependable, loyal, honest, and conscientious. (13)

interact. To act with others through communication and behavior. (1)

J–L

jealousy. Hostility toward someone believed to be a rival or toward someone getting special advantages. (5)

layoff. The process of firing people because positions have been cut. (22)

letter of resignation. Letter to your supervisor stating that you are leaving your job. (22)

loyalty. Quality of being faithful; *not* doing anything to harm a person or his or her reputation. (13)

M–O

mentor. Someone who makes an effort to help you learn and succeed on the job. (5)

merit. Actual quality of work based on facts. (5)

misinformation. Untrue or incomplete information. (10)

morale. Feelings and attitudes about the workplace. (8)

motive. Reason that explains a person's actions. (10)

mutually rewarding relationship. Relationship that is beneficial to both people. (20)

negative attitude. Belief or feeling that life is terrible and everything will be a disaster. (2)

negative reinforcement. Encouragement of negative attitudes. (9)

network. To make connections with people in the work world. (18)

nonverbal communication. Communication without words. (1, 12)

observational learning. Watching someone to learn how to do something. (13)

opportunity. Chance for success. (14)

orientation. Presentation that describes a company and its rules. (15)

output. Result of labor. (3)

overqualified. Having more knowledge and skills than a job requires. (8)

oversensitivity. Condition of taking slights and mistakes too personally and seriously. (6)

P–R

peer. Person working at the same job level. (4)

perfectionist. Someone who wants to do everything perfectly and dreads making a mistake. (19)

performance review. Formal evaluation of a worker's work and productivity. (15)

personality conflict. Discord between people, caused by their different temperaments. (20)

plateau. High, flat stretch of land; a period of time when things do not change. (17)

positive attitude. Belief or feeling that life is good and everything will turn out fine. (2)

prejudice. Hostility toward a group of people. (6)

priority. Something that is more important than other things. (14)

proactive. Taking action before requested or before a need arises. (7)

probation. Period of time during which you are on staff, but your performance is evaluated to determine whether you should stay or be let go. (15)

productivity. Measure of output, for example, the number of products produced per hour. (3)

professional organization. Organization or club established to help people be successful in a profession or career. (18)

racism. Prejudice based on race, skin color, or ethnic heritage. (6)

reduction in force (rif). The process of firing people because positions have been cut; another term for *layoff.* (22)

resign. To deliberately leave a position. (22)

role model. Person whose behavior is a good example and worth following. (18)

rumor. Widely spread information whose truth and source are unknown. (10)

rumor mill. Process in which people hear a rumor and pass it on, often adding misinformation. (10)

S–U

self-awareness. Being aware of how you are communicating and being aware of how people react to your communication and behavior. (1)

self-confident. The feeling of being sure of one's abilities. (14)

self-esteem. The feeling of self-worth; feeling self-confident. (14)

selfishness. Habit of putting one's own needs above those of others. (6)

service industry. Industry consisting of jobs that provide a service, such as serving food, cutting hair, fixing a car, or providing medical care. (6)

sexism. Prejudice based on gender. (6)

status quo. The way things are; the existing state of affairs. (15)

stress. Feeling of tension, strain, or pressure. (9)

subordinate. Person below you in rank. (5)

supervisor. Person who oversees your work. (5)

tardiness. Being late for work. (16)

team. Group of people who work together. (3)

team player. Worker whose actions help the team. (3)

teamwork. Working together to produce results. (3)

unprofessional. Acting in ways that do not meet the high standards of an excellent worker. (16)

unwritten rule. Rule everyone follows, but is not written down. (15)

V–Z

verbal aggression. Speaking in a hostile or angry way. (9)

verbal communication. Communication using words. (1, 12)

work attitude. Attitude toward work that has three components: attitude toward self, attitude toward work (work ethic), and attitude toward the workplace. (14)

work ethic. A person's attitude toward his or her job. (14)

written rule. Company's rule that appears in the employee handbook. (15)

Index

Notes

Notes

Notes

Notes

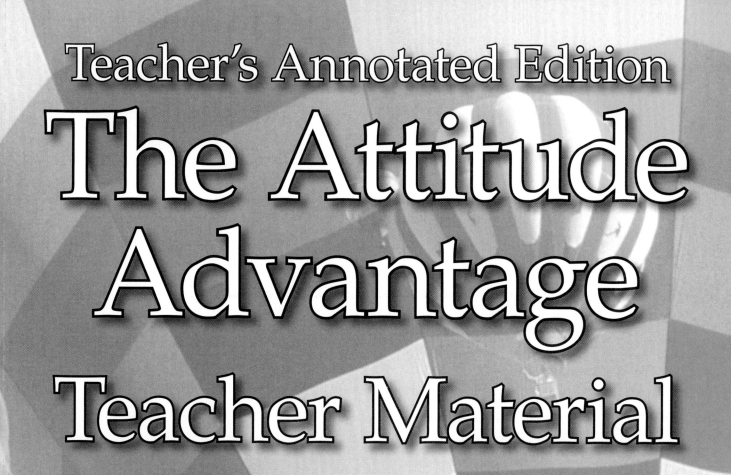

Teacher's Annotated Edition
The Attitude Advantage
Teacher Material

Contents

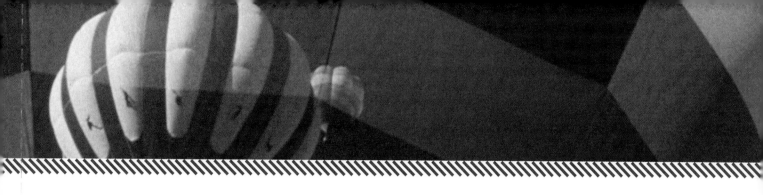

Introduction

If students have a positive and constructive attitude, they will have an advantage at work and in life. *The Attitude Advantage* student text is designed to help students cultivate positive and constructive attitudes. The *Teacher's Annotated Edition* provides answers to questions in the student text, as well as additional teacher material to help you and your students get the most from the text. The following information will help you use the student text and the *Teacher's Annotated Edition*.

Organization of the Student Text

The student text is designed to be engaging and easy to read. It is organized into small chunks of information that are easy to teach and easy for the students to absorb.

Parts

The 22 topics are organized into four parts. Each part covers several major concepts in human relations in the workplace.

- **Part 1:** introduces human relations skills and attitudes and describes the different kinds of worker relationships.
- **Part 2:** analyzes constructive and destructive attitudes at work and shows their impact on morale and productivity.
- **Part 3:** focuses on how to build good interpersonal relationships.
- **Part 4:** presents ways to learn from mistakes and repair damaged relationships. The final topic looks at positive ways to leave a job.

Topics

Each topic is organized into four easy-to-read and easy-to-understand sections. Attractive photographs enliven the pages and show diversity. Four large headers demarcate each section: *Discover, Analyze, Apply*, and *Review*. A fifth large header, *Discuss*, signals the discussion questions.

- **Discover:** a realistic case study. The complete case is presented on two facing pages (a spread), to create an appealing and compact visual image. The

spread includes the objectives for the topic, a complete case study, and stimulating questions under the *Discuss* header. At the top of the second page of each topic is a sentence that summarizes the key concept of the topic.

- **Analyze:** case analysis and concepts. This section is presented on the second spread in all topics, except in longer Topic 12. The section examines the key concepts of the topic and their relationship to the case. Key terms in the *Analyze* section are highlighted in bold and defined in the glossary at the back of the book. Each *Analyze* section has a set of stimulating questions under the *Discuss* header.
- **Apply:** a new case to which students can apply concepts learned in the *Analyze* section. Stimulating questions under the *Discuss* header help students think about the case and apply the concepts.
- **Review:** ten true/false questions and three to five short-answer questions. These questions give students the opportunity to review what they have learned.
- **Discuss:** critical-thinking questions. There are three sets of *Discuss* questions in each topic—after the *Discover, Analyze,* and *Apply* sections. These questions can be used as the basis of small-group or whole-class discussions. They can also be used as written assignments.

The *Teacher's Annotated Edition*

The *Teacher's Annotated Edition* provides complete support to the teacher in a compact, easy-to-use format. Answers to all questions in the student text are supplied right where they are posed. Sample answers are provided for questions that are open-ended so any teacher can use the text and be successful.

Following the student text is the "Teaching Materials" section, designated with "T" page numbers. This section contains teaching strategies to help you incorporate activities into your class sessions, and for each topic, a reproducible master to reinforce topic concepts.

Each topic has a strategy page. This page lists the objectives, terms, and key concept of the topic. The titles and page numbers of the two cases and of the reproducible master for the topic are also given. In addition, several activities are recommended to reinforce, enhance, or extend learning of the topic concept. These activities include the following:

- **Journal Writing:** provides students with the opportunity to reflect on concepts learned and apply them to their own experiences, in the privacy of their own journal. Journal writing also gives students another opportunity to improve their writing ability.
- **Cooperative Learning:** provides an opportunity to develop team skills. See "Working in Teams" on this page.
- **Research Topics and Speakers:** provide ways to extend learning beyond the classroom.

The reproducible activity masters provided for each topic are complete on one or two pages. These activities reinforce the concepts presented in the topic. Some are general activities, but most are self-assessments. The self-assessments ask students to apply the topic concept directly to themselves and evaluate their attitudes. Each self-assessment includes the following sections:

- **Activity:** Students answer questions by checking boxes.
- **Scoring:** Scores are determined by counting the number of checks in one of the columns.
- **Interpretation:** For each score or range, an interpretation is offered. Important note: The results are general and NOT definitive. The interpretation is mainly to suggest areas where students may need more work. For low scores, it is suggested that students talk with a teacher or counselor to discuss the subject, such as negative attitude.
- **Action:** For every self-assessment, ways to make improvements are suggested.

Using *The Attitude Advantage* in Class

Because of its organization and design, *The Attitude Advantage* is easy to use in class. You can use it as you would a traditional text, assigning topics and discussion questions as homework.

You can take advantage of the small sections of text, however, and use them when you have a few minutes of class time to fill. In 15 or 20 minutes, you can have the class work on the *Discover* and *Analyze*, or *Apply* and *Review* sections.

The Attitude Advantage also lends itself to cooperative learning and teamwork. See "Working in Teams" on this page.

A great way to make the cases come alive is to have students act them out. Students may be shy about acting, but the information in "Using Role Plays" will help you organize an acting/role-playing activity so everyone benefits and has fun. See page T6.

The Attitude Advantage is especially easy for substitute teachers to use when you are away from the classroom.

Protecting Students' Privacy

Human relations skills are best learned when applied by the student to himself or herself. However, in the classroom, teachers must protect the privacy of each student. In *The Attitude Advantage* student text, all questions focus on the cases or a general situation with which students may be familiar. Students should never be asked to share personal information or experiences in class.

The Attitude Advantage provides several ways for students to apply human relations concepts to their lives. First, the reproducible masters labeled "self-assessments" in the *Teacher's Annotated Edition* ask students to apply the concepts to their experiences. Second, the journal writing activities on the topic strategy pages give students another chance to reflect on their lives and their human relations.

Before students begin an activity, it is important to tell them which of their completed activities may be read by you or others, and which will remain confidential. Some teachers never collect journal entries, which allows these student writings to remain confidential. Other teachers let students know that activities will be kept in a locked cabinet and only the teacher will see them. In all other cases, inform students that their writings may be shared with others and, therefore, not kept confidential.

Teaching Strategies

This *Teaching Strategies* section consists of three articles to help you use *The Attitude Advantage* to reinforce concepts through teamwork, role plays, and building vocabulary.

Working in Teams

A key human relations skill is teamwork. We do our students a favor by teaching them how to work together in teams. Students can get practice working in teams through role plays and cooperative activities.

The first step in creating an effective team for any group activity is to help the team members feel comfortable with each other. This can be achieved through activities that help students get to know each other. The following activities are often used in corporate team training.

"Getting to Know You" Activities

- **I'd Like You to Meet . . . .** Organize students into pairs. Tell students the goal is to have each person introduce his or her partner so we can learn something about our classmates. They are to learn and share the following information about their partners: full name, nickname or preferred name (if appropriate), where they work if employed, which grade they are in (if it is a multigrade class), what school they are from (if it is a center with students from several schools), and a favorite hobby, book, movie, song, or band. Give students about four minutes, two apiece, to learn the information.

   Have each student introduce his or her partner. If you (the teacher) have partnered with a student, you and your partner should go first. If you are preparing a seating chart, write the name and preferred name of each student on your overhead seating chart. Have students do the same on their copies of the seating chart.

- **Birthday Game.** Have students get up from their seats. Tell them they cannot use any spoken or written words to communicate. Then tell them to put themselves in order by birth date (month and day). When the class is done, have each student say his or her birthday. Then discuss how difficult it was to communicate nonverbally. You might expand the discussion to communication in general and the methods used to communicate nonverbally.

Role Plays as Team Activities

   In addition to the benefits of playing a role, students must work together to create an effective role play. They must cooperate, share, compromise, and give feedback. If your students do not know each other well before a role-play activity, have them do one of the "Getting to Know You" activities. For more on how to use role plays, see the section, "Using Role Plays."

Cooperative Learning as Team Activities

   Cooperative learning groups and activities give students another opportunity to practice teamwork skills. During cooperative learning, students must use human relations skills to be effective.

   Each topic page in the *Teacher's Annotated Edition* offers one or more cooperative activities. The cooperative activities usually begin with the words, "organize students into groups." There are many ways to organize students into groups, but it is advisable to vary their composition periodically to let students work with a variety of different classmates. At least some of the time, groups should be mixed in terms of abilities and talents so there are opportunities for the students to learn from one another.

   In cooperative learning groups, students learn to work together toward a group goal. Each member is dependent on others for the outcome. This interdependence is a basic component of any cooperative learning group or work team. Students understand that one person cannot succeed unless everyone succeeds. The value of each group member is affirmed as learners work toward the group goal. This is true in business also. Everyone in the business, from the president to the maintenance staff, has critical work to do. Each person individually and as part of the group must perform well so the business can meet its goal.

   Another value of using small cooperative groups is that it gives more students a chance to participate. If you have a whole-class discussion, usually only three to five students speak. If you organize the class into small groups of three to five, each student will have a chance to speak. Students are also less likely to feel intimidated when speaking to a small group. They are more likely to share their ideas and take the risk to participate. To share all ideas or results, each group can elect someone to present the group's list to the class.

   You will need to monitor the effectiveness of the groups, intervening as necessary to provide task assistance or to help with interpersonal and group skills. At the conclusion of group activities, evaluate students' achievement and help them discuss how well they cooperated with each other and what they can do to improve their interactions the next time they work in a group.

Using Role Plays

   Role plays are an excellent way for students to practice human relations skills. Role playing allows students to practice solving problems and making decisions under nonthreatening circumstances and enables students to examine the feelings of others. Such activities also help students learn effective ways to react or cope when confronted with similar situations in their own work lives.

   To make role playing most effective and least threatening, follow the guidelines suggested below. Notice the recommendation that students do role plays in small groups with only one or two observers. By doing so, the amount of "stage fright" is significantly reduced. When every group has completed its role play, ask a group to volunteer to perform theirs for the whole class and use it as the basis of a whole-class discussion.

Successful Role Play

   A successful role play has three parts: preparation, performance, and analysis.

Preparation

1. Organize students into small groups. The best size is the number of roles plus one or two.

2. Have students read the case that will be used for the role play. For best results, have them take turns reading aloud in their small groups.

3. For each role in the case, have students write the name of the character and a brief description of the person and his or her problem.

4. The extra person or two will have the role of observer. The observer watches the role play and looks for the key issues, concepts, or behaviors. Have the group brainstorm what the observers should look for in the role play. Observers should look especially for evidence of positive constructive attitudes and negative destructive attitudes and their effects.

5. Have the group assign a role to each person. Have students think about and discuss how they should play their roles.

Performance

6. Have the students perform their role plays in their groups for their observers.

Analysis

7. Have the small groups analyze their role play. Ask the observers for their observations and feedback. Have the players share any feelings or insights gained from the role play. Have the group summarize what they have learned from the role play.

Extension

If time permits, have students switch roles and perform the role play and analysis again. Ask a group to volunteer to perform their role play for the class. Then have a whole-class discussion.

Time Frame

The amount of time necessary for a role play varies, depending on the topic and the students. A rough estimate is 20 minutes for preparation, 5 minutes for performance, and 5 to 10 minutes for analysis. If students switch roles and perform the role play again, allow another 10 minutes. If a group performs for the class with a discussion afterward, allow another 20 to 30 minutes.

Closure

After the role-play analysis, have each student write a reaction paper. Have them note the topic of the role play, then respond to the following questions:

1. How effective was your group in planning and executing the role play?

2. Which role or roles did you play?

3. What did you learn from the role play and discussion?

4. How will this information be useful to you in the future?

5. What is your opinion of the role play as a way to learn about human relations?

Building Vocabulary

Learning vocabulary is not the main purpose of *The Attitude Advantage*, yet knowing key terms will help students understand human relations and build their human relations skills.

For each topic, a few key terms are highlighted in bold in the student text and listed on the topic page in the *Teacher's Annotated Edition*. These terms are defined in the glossary at the back of the student text.

In preparation for the vocabulary-building activities, have students make a vocabulary notebook or designate a section of their regular notebook for vocabulary. Have them make a list of all the bold terms in the topic you are working on. For topics with few words, you might want to combine the lists from two or more topics.

Choose one or more of the vocabulary activities listed below for class prereading or postreading activities. The activities are labeled as *Individual* or *Group*, but the *Individual Activities* can also be used for small groups.

Individual Activities

- **Definition Predictions.** For each word on the list, write what you think the definition is. Compare your definition with the definition in the glossary. Write the word and its correct definition in your vocabulary notebook.

- **Your Own Definitions.** For each word on the list, write the definition in your own words. Use examples or diagrams to help you.

- **Sentences.** For each word on the list, find a sentence in the text that contains the word. Copy that sentence into your vocabulary notebook. Then write your own sentence that uses the word.

- **Words in the News.** Find an article on a subject covered in the topic. Look in newspapers, news magazines *(Time, Newsweek, US News and World Report)*, or business magazines *(Business Week, Fortune, Forbes, Nation's Business)*. Make a copy of the article, read it, and look for the words on the list. Circle any that you find. Copy each sentence with a circled word into your vocabulary notebook. Then rewrite each sentence in your own words.

- **Flash Cards.** You will need a stack of index cards. For each word on the list, write the word on one side of an index card and its definition on the other. Use the flash cards to test your knowledge. Use the word side to read the word, then tell the definition. Use the definition side to read the definition, then tell and spell the word.

- **Word Search.** Create a word search on a piece of graph paper. Use the words on the list. Make a copy without the answers to exchange with a partner.

- **Crossword Puzzle.** Create a crossword puzzle on a piece of graph paper. Use the words on the list. Be sure to number the words and include a definition for each word. Make a blank copy to exchange with a partner.

- **Fairy Tale.** Choose a nursery rhyme or fairy tale. Rewrite it in today's language and use the words on the list. Share your rewritten fairy tale.

- **Word Pairs.** Study the words on the list. Organize the words into pairs. (You can also use your flash-cards to pair the words.) On a sheet of paper, record your pairs. Then write a sentence or two explaining why you put the words together. Here are some ways that words can be related: same, similar, opposites, both words are part of the same thing, one word is part of the other word, one word is the result of the other word. For example, *positive attitude* and *negative attitude* are opposites.

Group Activities

- **Concentration.** This game works best for terms lists with eight or more terms. Organize students into groups. Give each group index cards equal to twice the number of terms. Have the group write each term on one card, then the definition for each term on another card. Have students place all cards face down, mix up the order, then arrange the cards neatly in rows. Have the group select one member as the monitor. Give the monitor the list of words with their correct definitions. Have students determine the order of play (clockwise, birth dates). The first student turns over one card and reads the word or definition. The student then turns over another card. If the word and definition match, the student takes the two cards. The monitor checks the list to make sure the term and definition are correct. If they do not match, the play passes to the next person. Play continues until all the cards are picked up. The person with the most cards wins.

- **What Was the Question?** This game is based on the game "Jeopardy." Organize students into groups. Have each group make a terms list with definitions. Organize the groups into pairs. Have one group read definitions to the other group. The other group must give the word in the form of a question, for example, "What is *teamwork*?"

- **Charades.** Write each term on a slip of paper. Place the slips in an envelope or bowl. Ask a volunteer to take a slip and act out the term. Have the class guess the term.

Topic 1
The Need for Human Relations Skills

Discover

- what human relations is.
- why you need human relations skills.
- how human relations skills help you on the job.

Terms

body language

communication

human relations

human relations skills

interact

nonverbal communication

self-awareness

verbal communication

Key Concept

Your success is influenced by how well you relate to others.

Cases

- *Who Is the Best Candidate?* page 8
- *Employee Personalities*, page 12

Reproducible Master

Activity: *With Whom Would You Interact?* page T10

Activities

1. **Terms** Choose one of the vocabulary-building activities listed on page T8.
2. **Journal Writing** Do you think human relations skills are important? Explain your answer.
3. **Journal Writing** Evaluate your own human relations skills. Are they good or poor? What do you think you need to improve?
4. **Cooperative Learning** Organize students into small groups. Have each group member list every person with whom he or she interacts in a day. Have members compare their lists. On average, what is the total number of people that each student interacts with in a day?
5. **Speaker** Invite one or a panel of industry representatives to discuss the importance of human relations in their industries.

Topic 1, Activity

With Whom Would You Interact?

Name_____ **Date**_____ **Period**_____

The chart below lists a variety of careers. If the career you are interested in isn't included, add it in the blank at the end of the chart. If you had a job in each career, with whom would you interact? Place a checkmark in the appropriate columns.

Career	Customers	Coworkers	Supervisor	People to Supervise	Upper Management	Others
Accountant						
Airline Flight Attendant						
Auto Mechanic						
Computer Programmer						
Construction Worker						
Customer Service Representative						
Hotel Front Desk Manager						
Medical Lab Technician						
Retail Salesperson						
Photographer						
Receptionist						
Salesclerk						
Secretary						
Stockbroker						
Telemarketer						

Topic 2
Your Attitude Counts

Discover

- the difference between a positive attitude and a negative one.
- how attitude affects behavior.
- how attitudes can change.

Terms

attitude

negative attitude

positive attitude

Key Concept

Your behavior is influenced by your attitude.

Cases

- *Who Has a Positive Attitude?* page 14
- *A New Coworker*, page 18

Reproducible Master

Self-Assessment: *What Is Your Attitude?* page T12

Activities

1. **Terms** Choose one of the vocabulary-building activities listed on page T8.
2. **Journal Writing** Describe one of your attitudes that has affected your human relations. Was the attitude positive or negative? What was the effect of this attitude? As you think about the situation now, what would you change?
3. **Journal Writing** What does it mean when an adult says you have "an attitude"? Describe a situation in which an adult has said it to you or about someone else. What did the adult mean? What did the adult want you or the other person to do? Do you think your attitude was negative?
4. **Cooperative Learning** Organize students into small groups. Have each group list all the people they can think of with positive attitudes, then list all the people they can think of with negative attitudes. They can include people on TV, in movies, and characters in books. Have the group list the qualities that all the positive people have, then all the qualities that the negative people have. To extend the activity, have two groups join together and compare their lists. Have them discuss whether they agree or disagree with the category for the people on each list.
5. **Speaker** Invite a police officer to discuss situations in which people are approached by an officer and how attitude influences the outcome.

Topic 2, Self-Assessment

What Is Your Attitude?

Name_____ Date_____ Period_____

A person's attitude is complex. In addition, a person can change his or her attitude. The following quiz will just give you some insight into your attitude today. For each pair of statements, check the one that best describes you. Respond honestly.

A	Statement A	B	Statement B
	A. I listen to other people's ideas and weigh all sides in a discussion.		**B.** Other people's ideas are not as good as mine, so I don't usually give them much weight.
	A. I need to gather as many facts as possible before forming my opinions.		**B.** I know where I stand on most issues, so I have no need to explore the pros and cons.
	A. I feel comfortable speaking in front of a group to share my thoughts and opinions.		**B.** I am nervous speaking in front of a group. I feel that my opinion is not important to others.
	A. I enjoy meeting new people, both on the job and in social situations.		**B.** I avoid situations where I don't know most of the people.
	A. I try to understand the feelings of others and to respond to their needs.		**B.** It is impossible to understand every person, so I don't bother.
	A. I am patient with difficult people and try to work things out.		**B.** It's impossible to please difficult people, so I don't even try.
	A. I believe it is my responsibility as an employee to be loyal, even if I dislike my job or my boss.		**B.** A bad boss or a bad job deserves neither my respect nor my loyalty.
	A. I would never take what isn't mine, whether it is company property or time from the job.		**B.** Taking a few office supplies or an extra sick day isn't stealing. Companies expect it and budget for it.
	A. I am comfortable working with people who do not share my values, beliefs, or background.		**B.** I am uncomfortable working with people who do not share my values, beliefs, or background.
	A. Having a good sense of humor is helpful when dealing with people on the job.		**B.** Work is serious business, and humor is out of place.
	Total A's:		**Total B's:**

(Continued)

What Is Your Attitude? (*Continued*)

Name_____

Scoring

For each checkmark in the A column, give yourself one point. The checkmarks in the B column get no points.

My total score is _____.

Interpretation

Score	Meaning
9 or 10	Congratulations! Your positive attitude will help you in any career you choose.
7 or 8	Your attitude is basically positive, but could be better. You need to improve your attitude in one or two areas.
5 or 6	Your attitude is split between positive and negative and may be causing you problems. You need to improve your attitude in several areas.
4 or less	Your attitude is mostly negative and is probably causing you problems. Your attitude may also keep you from achieving success. You need to improve your attitude in many areas.

Action

It is always a good idea to work on improving your attitudes; but the lower your score, the more work you need to do. Below, list the problem areas you need to work on. For each problem area, describe one way to improve. Focus on one area for at least a week. When you have improved in that area, work on another. Continue until you think you have improved in all your problem areas. If your score is 6 or below, you might want to meet with a teacher or counselor to discuss ways to improve your attitude.

Ways to Improve My Attitude

_____
_____
_____
_____
_____
_____
_____
_____
_____
_____
_____
_____
_____
_____
_____
_____
_____

Topic 3
Teamwork

Discover

- the value of teamwork in the workplace.
- the human relations skill of cooperation.
- how a good attitude can improve teamwork.

Terms

cooperation

output

productivity

team

team player

teamwork

Key Concept

When people work well together, everyone profits.

Cases

- *Why Did the Team Improve?* page 20
- *How to Get Ahead,* page 24

Reproducible Master

Activity: *Team Challenge*, page T15

Activities

1. **Terms** Choose one of the vocabulary-building activities listed on page T8.
2. **Journal Writing** Name a team or a group to which you belong. Describe your relationship with one of the members of the team and how it affected your team's productivity.
3. **Journal Writing** What talents do you bring to a team?
4. **Cooperative Learning** Organize the class into small groups. Have each group describe three situations that illustrate cooperation. Choose one of the situations and change it so that it shows the opposite of cooperation. Have each group present its "opposite of cooperation" situation. After each presentation, have the class offer suggestions of how the situation could be changed to show cooperation. After all groups are done, have the class discuss the importance of cooperation.
5. **Speaker** Invite the captain of a sports team and/or the debate team, the chair of a committee, and a businessperson to discuss what teamwork is and how important it is to team success.

Topic 3, Activity

Team Challenge

Name_____ **Date**_____ **Period**_____

How can you work the most efficiently in a team? Try this activity to find out.

Procedure

1. You will be assigned to a team.
2. Your team will make as many perfectly formed boxes as possible.
3. Use the box template provided by your teacher. (See page T16.)
4. Each team will get scissors, glue or tape, and pencils.
5. Each team will get an unlimited supply of box material (white paper).
6. You will have 10 minutes to make your boxes.
7. When time is up, the teacher will perform a quality control check, and tell you how many boxes were acceptable.

Questions

1. How many boxes did your team produce? _____
2. How many acceptable boxes did your team produce? _____
3. Describe the quality of your boxes._____

   _____

4. How well did your group work together?_____
5. What, if any, problems did you have getting along and performing the tasks? _____

   _____

   _____

   _____

   _____

6. Did your group choose a leader? Why or why not? _____

   _____

7. Did each team member make complete boxes, or did you divide up the tasks (specialize)? _____

   _____

8. What strategies did the winning team use? _____

   _____

9. How could you improve the efficiency of your team? _____

   _____

10. Make a list of recommendations for how to work well on a team. _____

    _____

    _____

    _____

    _____

Topic 3, Activity

Box Template

DIRECTIONS: Cut on solid lines, and fold on dotted lines.

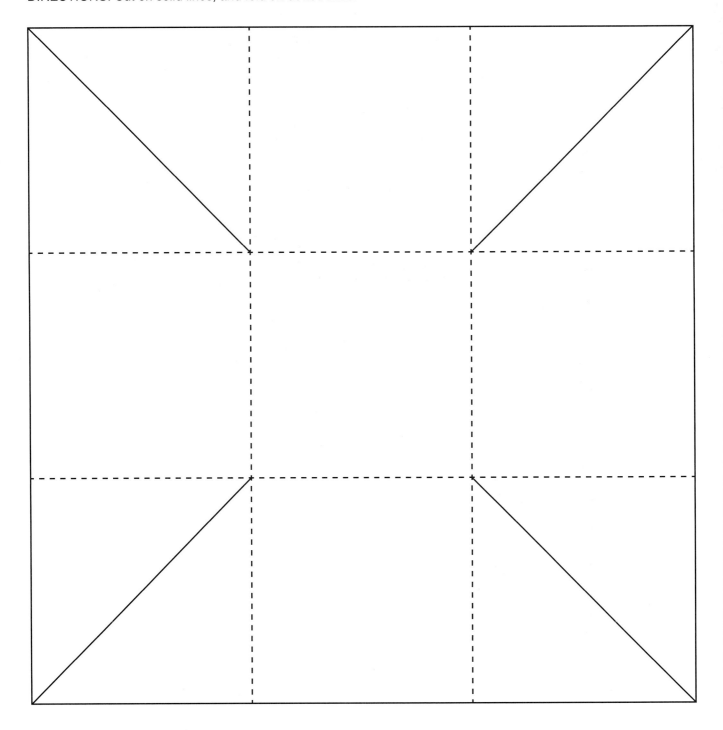

Topic 4
Coworker Relationships

Discover

- what a good work relationship is.
- how relationships at work affect your happiness and success.
- how relationships affect each other.

Terms

coworker

impartial

peer

Key Concept

Good communication can improve coworker relationships.

Cases

- *The Resentful Coworker*, page 26
- *Working with Slackers*, page 30

Reproducible Master

Self-Assessment: *How Do You Relate to Coworkers?* page T18

Activities

1. **Terms** Choose one of the vocabulary-building activities listed on page T8.
2. **Journal Writing** Think of a relationship you have with a coworker, classmate, or teammate. Is the relationship good or bad? Give your evidence. How does this relationship affect your effectiveness at work, in school, or on the team? If the relationship is causing problems, what can you do to improve it?
3. **Cooperative Learning** Organize students into small groups. Ask each group to describe three situations in which it is important to be impartial. Choose one of the situations and change it so that it shows the opposite of impartiality. Have each group present its "opposite of impartiality" situation. After each presentation, have the class offer suggestions of how the situation could be changed to show impartiality. After all groups are done, have the class discuss how to be impartial.
4. **Speaker** Invite the person in charge of the food preparation crew at a fast-food restaurant. Have that person describe how teamwork and coworker relationships are important to the job and how new crew members are trained to be good team members. That person might also describe what can happen if coworkers do not get along on the job.

Topic 4, Self-Assessment

How Do You Relate to Coworkers?

Name_____ **Date**_____ **Period**_____

Choose two people with whom you have worked on a job or at school. They should be at the same level as you. Coworker *A* should be a person with whom you have a good relationship. Coworker *B* should be a person with whom you have a poor relationship. Read each of the statements in the following table. For each coworker, answer yes or no in the appropriate column.

Statement	Coworker *A* (good relationship)	Coworker *B* (poor relationship)
A good relationship with this person is important to me.		
My productivity depends on my relationship with this person.		
I lose my patience with this person.		
I think it is his or her responsibility to make the first move.		
Our supervisor favors me over this person.		
Our supervisor favors this person over me.		
This person often complains.		
This person has a positive attitude.		
This person pulls his or her own weight.		
This person shares my sense of humor.		
We are about the same age.		
We can discuss problems honestly.		
We have similar backgrounds.		
We have similar beliefs and values.		
We have the same interests and lifestyle.		

Analysis

1. Compare your answers for Coworker *A* with your answers for Coworker *B*. Circle the statements for which you answered differently for each coworker.

2. From these differences, why do you think you have more trouble relating to Coworker *B*?

_____

_____

_____

Action

What can you do to improve your relationship with Coworker *B*? Describe one action you could take.

Ways to Improve My Coworker Relationships

_____

_____

_____

_____

_____

Topic 5
Relationships with Supervisors

Discover

- the nature of supervisor-employee relationships.
- how good coworker and supervisor relationships interact.
- the impact of supervisor-subordinate relationships on worker attitudes and productivity.

Terms

favoritism

jealousy

mentor

merit

subordinate

supervisor

Key Concept

Relationships with supervisors affect your work success and coworker relationships.

Cases

- *The Problem of Favoritism*, page 32
- *New Job, New Supervisor*, page 36

Reproducible Master

Self-Assessment: *How Do You Communicate with Supervisors?* page T20

Activities

1. **Terms** Choose one of the vocabulary-building activities listed on page T8.
2. **Journal Writing** Describe your attitude toward supervisors or people in authority, such as a teacher, workplace supervisor, team captain, parent, or president of a club. Do you think your attitude is helpful to you? If not, what could you change?
3. **Journal Writing** What is your opinion of favoritism on the job or in school? Is it ever beneficial? If you have every shown favoritism to someone, explain why. Describe a situation in which you have experienced favoritism or been affected by favoritism shown to someone else. What is the best way to handle favoritism?
4. **Speaker** Invite someone who is a supervisor at his or her job. Ask that person to describe his or her job in terms of the supervisor's responsibilities. If appropriate, consider asking a supervisor from the school food service or maintenance staff.

Topic 5, Self-Assessment

How Do You Communicate with Supervisors?

Name_____ Date_____ Period_____

How well do you communicate with your teachers, supervisors, or others in authority? The following quiz can give you some insight. Think of a situation in which you are the subordinate. Read each statement below. Check the "Agree" column if you agree. Check the "Disagree" column if you disagree.

Agree	Disagree	Statements
		1. If I don't understand what is expected of me, I ask for more information.
		2. I don't feel embarrassed when I need to ask for help.
		3. I expect to earn the rewards of working by doing a good job.
		4. I welcome having others criticize my work and point out how to improve it.
		5. I am willing to ask how I can improve my performance.
		6. I make it clear that I have personal goals and ambitions.
		7. I know how to tactfully say I disagree during a discussion with someone in authority.
		8. When my supervisor asks for my opinions, I am able to give them.
		9. If I am having a problem that affects my work, I can discuss it with my supervisor.
		10. I understand the difference between a good working relationship and a friendship.

Scoring

Count the number of statements for which you checked the "Agree" column. This number is your score.

My score is _____.

Interpretation

Score	Meaning
10	Congratulations! You have almost perfect communication with your supervisor.
8 or 9	Your communication is good.
6 or 7	Your communication is average, but could be improved.
5 or less	You need to work on ways to improve your communication.

(Continued)

Topic 5, Self-Assessment

How Do You Communicate with Supervisors? (*Continued*)

Name_____

Action

It is always a good idea to work on improving your communication; but the lower your score, the more work you need to do. Below, list the problem areas you need to work on. For each problem area, describe one way to improve. Focus on one area for at least a week. When you have improved in that area, work on another. Continue until you think you have improved in all your problem areas. If your score is 5 or less, you might want to meet with a teacher or counselor to discuss ways to improve your communication.

Ways to Improve Your Communication with Supervisors

_____

_____

_____

_____

_____

_____

_____

_____

_____

_____

_____

_____

_____

_____

_____

_____

_____

_____

_____

_____

_____

_____

_____

_____

_____

_____

_____

_____

Topic 6
Destructive Attitudes

Discover

- the nature of destructive attitudes.
- the negative effect of destructive attitudes on the job.
- types of destructive attitudes.

Terms

ageism

bigot

discrimination

dissatisfaction

oversensitivity

prejudice

racism

selfishness

service industry

sexism

Key Concept

The most productive worker in the world will not find career success with a bad attitude.

Cases

- *The Too-Efficient Waitress*, page 40
- *You and the Malcontents*, page 44

Reproducible Master

Self-Assessment: *Are Your Attitudes Destructive?* page T23

Activities

1. **Terms** Choose one of the vocabulary-building activities listed on page T8.
2. **Activity** Use the Topic 6 Self-Assessment, "Are Your Attitudes Destructive?" as the basis for students to evaluate each other. Have students work in pairs. Have each student rate his or her partner, then compare the partner's rating with the student's rating of himself or herself. Does the partner's rating agree with the student's own rating? Is there a big difference? How do you explain the difference? If your attitudes are more destructive than you thought, what changes could you make to improve your attitudes?
3. **Journal Writing** Think about a destructive attitude of yours or a peer's. What impact has it had on your job or studies?
4. **Journal Writing** Answer these questions, which were posed in the *Analyze* section of the text: Do I get angry or rude to people for no obvious reason? Am I oversensitive about certain matters? Am I dissatisfied or negative about anything? If you answered yes to any of these questions, use your journal to explore your answers. Write why you get angry, are oversensitive, or are negative. Write about ways you could lessen or resolve your anger, oversensitivity, or negativity.
5. **Research** Have students research a law established to protect people from discrimination, for example, Equal Pay Act, Civil Rights Act, Age Discrimination Employment Act, or Americans with Disabilities Act.

Topic 6, Self-Assessment

Are Your Attitudes Destructive?

Name_____ Date_____ Period_____

Which of the following words describe your attitude? For each word, rate yourself on the following scale:

5 = always, 4 = often, 3 = sometimes, 2 = rarely, I = never

Then, go back through the list. If the word describes a constructive attitude, put your rating in the "Constructive" column. If the word describes a destructive attitude, put your rating in the "Destructive" column. There are five constructive words and five destructive words.

Attitudes	Your Rating	Constructive	Destructive
accepting			
angry			
dissatisfied			
helpful			
loyal			
oversensitive			
polite			
prejudiced			
selfish			
sincere			
		Total:	Total:

Scoring

Add the ratings for the words in the *Constructive* column.

My score for constructive attitude is _____.

Add the ratings for the words in the *Destructive* column.

My score for the destructive attitude is _____.

Now subtract your destructive score from you constructive score.
(Constructive score – Destructive score = Final score)

My final score is _____.

Interpretation

Score	Meaning
25	Perfect score! You have a great attitude!
15 to 24	Your attitude is good.
0 to 14	Your attitude is okay, but could be much better.
Less than 0	Your attitude is mostly destructive and could be interfering with your chance of success.

(Continued)

Are Your Attitudes Destructive? (*Continued*)

Name_____

Action

It is always a good idea to work on improving your attitude; but the lower your score, the more work you need to do. Below, list the problem areas you need to work on. For each problem area, describe one way to improve. Focus on one area for at least a week. When you have improved in that area, work on another. Continue until you think you have improved in all your problem areas. If your score is 14 or less, you might want to meet with a teacher or counselor to discuss ways to improve your attitude.

Ways to Change My Destructive Attitudes

_____
_____
_____
_____
_____
_____
_____
_____
_____
_____
_____
_____
_____
_____
_____
_____
_____
_____
_____
_____
_____
_____
_____
_____
_____

Topic 7
Constructive Attitudes

Discover

- what a constructive attitude is.
- the difference between a positive attitude and a constructive attitude.

Terms

constructive attitude

goodwill

proactive

Key Concept

A constructive attitude is more than just a smile.

Cases

- *Employee of the Month*, page 46
- *Handling a Bad Day*, page 50

Reproducible Master

Activity: *Developing Constructive Attitudes*, page T26

Activities

1. **Terms** Choose one of the vocabulary-building activities listed on page T8.
2. **Journal Writing** Recall a recent experience with someone who had a constructive attitude. Describe the attitude and the result of the person's behavior.
3. **Journal Writing** Describe one of your constructive attitudes and how it helped you in your work, in a relationship, or at school.
4. **Cooperative Learning** Organize students into small groups. Have each group describe three actions a business has taken to create goodwill. (They can be three actions by one business, or three actions by three different businesses.) The actions may be experienced personally or reported in the media. Discuss whether the actions were successful in creating goodwill. How did these actions affect the business? For a whole-class discussion, have each group present one action and ask the class to choose the most effective one.

Topic 7, Activity

Developing Constructive Attitudes

Name_____ **Date**_____ **Period**_____

It is hard to have a constructive attitude all the time. The goal is to respond to situations with a constructive attitude as often as possible. Five situations are described in the chart. For each one, give an example of how you responded (or could respond) with a constructive attitude. Then give an example of how you responded (or could respond) with a destructive attitude.

Situation	Constructive Response	Destructive Response
1. You missed the bus.		
2. Your project is behind schedule because some of your team members cannot find the information they need.		
3. One of the weaker players on the team makes a basket.		
4. You see someone approaching the doorway at the same time as you are. That person's hands are full.		
5. You got a lower grade than you expected, and your mother yelled at you for forgetting to wash the dishes.		

Topic 8
Morale

Discover

- what morale is.
- how high morale can lead to success at work.
- how low morale can lead to problems at work.

Terms

confidence

morale

overqualified

Key Concept

Morale influences success at work.

Cases

- *The Perfect Job*, page 52
- *An Insecure Job*, page 56

Reproducible Master

Activity: *How Can You Improve Morale?* page T28

Activities

1. **Terms** Choose one of the vocabulary-building activities listed on page T8.
2. **Journal Writing** Can you remember a situation, either in school or on a job, when your morale has been low? How did your low morale affect your productivity and your happiness?
3. **Journal Writing** Confidence is an important element of morale. How confident are you? What adds or subtracts from your feelings of confidence? What could you do to improve your confidence?
4. **Research** Southwest Airlines is famous for building high morale on the job. Research the company and write a report on what it does to keep morale high.
5. **Research** Have students search the phrase "morale in the workplace" on the Internet to learn about common morale problems and what people do to improve them. Have each student write a brief paper on one morale problem and its solution.

Topic 8, Activity

How Can You Improve Morale?

Name_____ **Date**_____ **Period**_____

The morale of any group can affect the efficiency and happiness of its members. Choose a group that you are part of or have observed. Possibilities include your workplace, school, a club, a store that you go to often, or a sports team. Then answer the following questions.

1. Describe the group that you chose. _____
    _____

2. Is the morale of this group good or poor?_____

3. List the evidence you used as the basis for your evaluation of the morale. For example, smiling workers would indicate good morale. Rudeness to customers would indicate poor morale. _____
    _____
    _____
    _____
    _____
    _____

4. If the morale is good, list the factors that encourage good morale. For example, nice decor would encourage good morale._____
    _____
    _____
    _____
    _____

5. If the morale is poor, list the factors that might be causing poor morale. For example, a dark, cramped workplace might cause poor morale. _____
    _____
    _____
    _____
    _____

6. Do you think each group member shares the overall morale of the group? What might be going on that you cannot see? _____
    _____
    _____
    _____
    _____

Copyright by Goodheart-Willcox Co., Inc.

Topic 9
Handling Stress on the Job

Discover

- the relationship between stress and aggression.
- the role of attitude in lowering your level of stress.
- how to deal with stress.

Terms

aggressive behavior

negative reinforcement

stress

verbal aggression

Key Concept

Stress is a normal part of life.

Cases

- *The Stressed-Out Manager*, page 58
- *The Delayed Promotion*, page 62

Reproducible Master

Self-Assessment: *How Do You Handle Stress?*
page T30

Activities

1. **Terms** Choose one of the vocabulary-building activities listed on page T8.
2. **Journal Writing** Write about a situation that is causing you stress. What is causing the stress? What are you doing to reduce the stress? If your reaction is destructive, how could you make your reaction constructive? If you are not doing anything, what ways could you try to reduce the stress?
3. **Cooperative Learning** Organize students into groups. Have each group describe three stressful situations at work, home, or school. For each situation, describe three destructive responses and three constructive responses. For each response, describe the likely impact on others.
4. **Discuss** How can negative reinforcement increase stress?
5. **Research** Search the term "stress management" on the Internet. Find an article that describes a useful way to deal with stress. Write a report on that article. Would you use this method? Why or why not?

Topic 9, Self-Assessment

How Do You Handle Stress?

Name_____ **Date**_____ **Period**_____

Everyone experiences stress at some time, and the best way to handle stress varies with the situation. This quiz can give you some insight into the way you cope with stress. Below is a list of ways to handle stress on the job. Read each reaction. If the reaction is positive, place a check in the positive column. If the reaction is negative, place a check in the negative column. Then circle each reaction that you have experienced.

Reaction to Stress	Positive thinking or action	Negative thinking or action
Blame your job.		
Blame yourself.		
Clean your desk drawers or something else.		
Clench your fists.		
Complain, complain, complain.		
Confide in a trusted friend.		
Count to ten silently.		
Daydream about your ideal job (or other situation).		
Eat candy or something else unhealthy.		
Give others the silent treatment.		
Go out for a walk.		
Leave for home early.		
Plan your revenge.		
Send a nasty e-mail, note, or letter.		
Slam a door.		
Swear under your breath.		
Tackle a task you have been avoiding.		
Take a coffee break.		
Talk about your problem so everyone can hear.		
Threaten to quit.		

Scoring

Count the number of positive reactions you circled.

   My positive score is _____.

Count the number of negative reactions you circled.

   My negative score is _____.

Interpretation

   Even though many negative reactions are common, any of them can cause problems at work or personally. You goal should be to change as many negative responses as possible to positive responses.

(Continued)

Topic 9, Self-Assessment

How Do You Handle Stress? (*Continued*)

Name_____

Action

Choose three of your negative reactions. If you did not have any negative reactions, choose three negative reactions from the list. For each reaction, give a suggestion for a better way to react.

Negative Reaction 1:_____

A Better Way to React: _____

_____

_____

_____

_____

_____

_____

_____

_____

Negative Reaction 2:_____

A Better Way to React: _____

_____

_____

_____

_____

_____

_____

_____

_____

Negative Reaction 3:_____

A Better Way to React: _____

_____

_____

_____

_____

_____

_____

_____

_____

Topic 10
Rumors

Discover

- the negative impact of rumors on the job.
- the role of attitude in the development and passing of rumors.
- how to avoid the rumor mill.

Terms

confidential information

gossip

misinformation

motive

rumor

rumor mill

Key Concept

One rumor can negatively affect a large group of people.

Cases

- *The Rumor Mill*, page 64
- *New Manager, Many Rumors*, page 68

Reproducible Master

Activity: *Consequences of the Rumor Mill*, page T33

Activities

1. **Terms** Choose one of the vocabulary-building activities listed on page T8.
2. **Journal Writing** Have you ever participated in a rumor mill? Describe the situation and how you participated. Did the rumor mill cause any harm or discomfort to anyone? Would you mind if the rumor mill spread rumors about you?
3. **Cooperative Learning** Organize students into small groups. First have the groups describe how the rumor mill works at school. Then have them give an example of a rumor that went around, the impact of the rumor, and what the true situation was. Ask each group to identify ways to stop the rumor mill. How would stopping the rumor mill have improved the situation? Have a group volunteer to share their example, and have the whole class discuss how to avoid the rumor mill. You might have the class develop a poster of ways to avoid participating in the rumor mill.
4. **Research** Have students research the role of rumors in English literature, financial markets, or politics. Those interested in military history might research the British rumor campaign during World War II.

Topic 10, Activity

Consequences of the Rumor Mill

Name_____ Date_____ Period_____

When misinformation or incomplete information hits the company rumor mill, there can be serious negative consequences. Assume that you are an employee who, while doing your job, overhears the following statements. What might happen if you passed that information along via the rumor mill? For each rumor, describe what might happen.

Rumor	Consequences of Spreading This Rumor
1. "The company president has been meeting with Conglomerated Industries. The last time CI took over a company, they fired a lot of staff."	
2. "I know the new manager seems like a really nice guy, but I heard that he left his last job under a cloud."	
3. "We lost a really big contract. It's all very hush-hush. I hear the top managers are meeting to decide the department's future."	
4. "I heard that the president doesn't like the new foodservice company for the cafeteria."	
5. "The new supervisor used to be a fashion model."	

Topic 11
Accepting Responsibility

Discover

- the importance of accepting responsibility for your actions.
- the importance of taking action to correct mistakes.

Terms

accepting responsibility

consequence

Key Concept

People who accept responsibility have a positive impact on those around them.

Cases

- *The Tardy Worker*, page 70
- *Someone Else's Mistake*, page 74

Reproducible Master

Activity: *Taking Responsibility*, page T35

Activities

1. **Terms** Choose one of the vocabulary-building activities listed on page T8.
2. **Journal Writing** Do you accept responsibility for your actions? If yes, give examples of the ways you accept responsibility. What effect does accepting responsibility have on others?
3. **Journal Writing** Give an example of a situation in which a person you know avoided accepting responsibility. (You can keep the person nameless by using "Miss X" or "Mr. Y" in your journal.) What was the result? What could that person have done to act more responsibly?
4. **Cooperative Learning** Organize students into groups. Have the groups list common excuses for being late, turning in work late, getting a poor grade, and so on. For each excuse, ask them to write a response that takes responsibility for the problem and an action the person should take to avoid the problem again.
5. **Journal Writing** Describe a time when someone who was working with you did not accept responsibility or did not act responsibly. How did you feel? What did you do?

Topic 11, Activity

Taking Responsibility

Name_____ **Date**_____ **Period**_____

How can you tell whether someone is taking responsibility for his or her actions? Read the following statements. Which ones were made by a person who is accepting responsibility for his or her actions? Place a check in the Yes or No column for each statement. In the last column, write what you think the response of the supervisor or peers would be.

Responsible?			
Yes	**No**	**Statement**	**Likely Response**
		1. "You'd be late for work, too, if you had to take two buses every morning."	
		2. "Oh no, we're out of paper. I should have ordered more last week."	
		3. "Nobody ever showed me the right way to do it. Am I supposed to be a mind reader?"	
		4. "I should have given you clearer directions."	
		5. "You promised to help me. It's your fault I missed the deadline."	
		6. "I thought I knew what to do. I'll work through lunch to fix this, and next time I'll ask for help sooner."	
		7. "She's a good teacher— I just didn't study enough for the exam."	
		8. "He distracted me. That's why I made the mistake."	

Topic 12
Communication

Discover

- how good communication skills help you build positive relationships at work.
- how a positive attitude helps you be an effective communicator.
- how nonverbal communication affects messages.

Terms

Note: These terms were first introduced in Topic 1.

communication

nonverbal communication

verbal communication

Key Concept

Career success depends on good communication.

Cases

- *The Very Bad, Terrible, Horrible First Day*, page 78
- *Face-to-Face vs. Electronic Communication*, page 82

Reproducible Master

Self-Assessment: *How Well Do You Communicate?*
page T37

Activities

1. **Terms** Choose one of the vocabulary-building activities listed on page T8.
2. **Journal Writing** What role does communication play in your life? With whom do you communicate most? Is there someone with whom you want or need to communicate more? Which communication skills would you like to improve?
3. **Activity** Ask everyone in the room to "freeze." Then, using appropriate discretion, give feedback on what students' nonverbal communication is telling you. (This activity only works once.) Have a class discussion on what different nonverbal behaviors communicate. You might have the class make a "nonverbal dictionary" of actions and their usual interpretations.
4. **Research** Culture affects the meaning of nonverbal behavior. For example, in America, looking someone in the eye while speaking to the person is an expected behavior. In Japan, such behavior is considered rude. Have students choose an aspect of nonverbal behavior in other cultures to research. They might choose a common behavior and research what it means in other cultures.

Topic 12, Self-Assessment

How Well Do You Communicate?

Name_____ Date_____ Period_____

How well do you communicate with others? The following quiz can give you some insight into your communication skills. For each pair of statements, check the one that best describes you. Respond honestly.

A	Statement A	B	Statement B
	A. I feel comfortable asking a coworker or fellow student for help with a work problem or school assignment.		**B.** I have a hard time asking others for help.
	A. I feel confident approaching a person in authority for help or to present an idea.		**B.** Speaking to people in authority is hard for me. I don't feel comfortable talking about my ideas or asking for help.
	A. I explain things well. People understand what I am saying.		**B.** People often misunderstand me when I am trying to make a point.
	A. I look others in the eye when I am explaining something.		**B.** I usually look elsewhere in order to think more easily about what I want to say.
	A. In a group or at a meeting, I feel comfortable expressing my opinions and sharing ideas.		**B.** I don't share my opinions in front of a group and dread being asked how I feel about an issue.
	A. People feel comfortable talking to me.		**B.** People rarely start conversations with me.
	A. I listen carefully when someone is asking me a question.		**B.** I often find myself thinking about how I will answer a question, rather than listening carefully.
	A. I think about how I am coming across when I talk on the telephone.		**B.** I rarely give thought to how I am communicating on the phone.
	A. I feel comfortable expressing myself in writing.		**B.** I would prefer to talk to someone, rather than write a letter or e-mail.
	A. I use my tone of voice to communicate interest in what another person is saying.		**B.** I tend to speak in a monotone.
	Total A's:		**Total B's:**

(Continued)

Topic 12, Self-Assessment

How Well Do You Communicate? (*Continued*)

Name_____

Scoring

For each checkmark in the A column, give yourself one point. The checkmarks in the B column get no points.

My total score is _____.

Interpretation

Score	Meaning
9 or 10	Congratulations! Your have effective communication skills that will help you in any career you choose.
7 or 8	Your communication skills are good, but they could be better.
5 or 6	Your communication skills are only fair.
4 or less	Your communication skills are poor. They may interfere with your job performance and success.

Action

It is always a good idea to work on improving your communication skills; but the lower your score, the more work you need to do. Below, list the problem areas you need to work on. For each problem area, describe one way to improve. Focus on one area for at least a week. When you have improved in that area, work on another. Continue until you think you have improved in all your problem areas. If your score is 4 or less, you might want to meet with a teacher or counselor to discuss ways to improve your communication skills.

Ways to Improve My Communication

_____

_____

_____

_____

_____

_____

_____

_____

_____

_____

_____

_____

_____

_____

_____

_____

Topic 13
Your Attitude and Job Success

Discover

- how to learn through observation.
- traits that form a constructive attitude.
- the role of a constructive attitude in career success.

Terms

conscientiousness

dependability

honesty

initiative

integrity

loyalty

observational learning

Key Concept

Integrity and initiative will put you on the path to success.

Cases

- *Learning by Observing*, page 84
- *How to Bring Costs Down*, page 88

Reproducible Master

Self-Assessment: *Are You a Valuable Employee?*
page T40

Activities

1. **Terms** Choose one of the vocabulary-building activities listed on page T8.
2. **Journal Writing** Identify five traits that give you a constructive attitude. What additional traits would you like to acquire?
3. **Journal Writing** How has a positive, constructive attitude made you more successful in school or work? What helps you maintain a positive attitude?
4. **Cooperative Learning** Organize students into groups. Have each group answer this question: If you were the captain of a team, what traits would you want in your team members and why? Have each group share its list with the class. Have the class compile a list of the most important traits.
5. **Cooperative Learning** Organize students into groups. Have each group make a list of skills that are best learned by observational learning. Have each group share an example.

Topic 13, Self-Assessment

Are You a Valuable Employee?

Name_____ Date_____ Period_____

Evaluate the personal qualities that make you a valuable employee. Rate yourself on each quality in the list. Use the following scale:

5 = always, 4 = usually, 3 = sometimes, 2 = rarely, l = never

Dependability

_____ My supervisor/teachers can count on me to do a job/assignment correctly.

_____ When I have a scheduled time to be someplace, I arrive on time.

_____ I do my share of every job/group project.

Loyalty

_____ I avoid making negative comments about other people.

_____ Secrets are safe with me.

_____ I refuse to gossip or spread rumors.

_____ I remain true to my ideals.

Honesty

_____ If I am paid to do a job, I make sure I put in the time expected.

_____ I do not use the personal property of others without permission.

_____ I use company equipment and supplies only for company business, never for my personal use.

Conscientiousness

_____ I do my work without needing to be closely supervised.

_____ I take pride in my work.

_____ I know what is expected of me.

Initiative

_____ I try to do just a little bit more than is expected.

_____ I am eager to learn new things.

_____ I make suggestions that will help others even if I don't directly benefit.

(Continued)

Topic 13, Self-Assessment

Are You a Valuable Employee? (*Continued*)

Name_____

Scoring

Add the numbers on each line to get a total. This total is your score.

My total score is _____.

Interpretation

Score	Meaning
75 or greater	Congratulations! You have nearly all the qualities of the ideal employee.
64 to 74	You have many qualities of the ideal employee, but are inconsistent in some areas.
48 to 63	You know what is expected, but are inconsistent in many areas.
32 to 47	You lack many of the qualities of the ideal employee.
Less than 32	You lack most of the qualities of the ideal employee.

Action

It is always a good idea to work on improving your qualities; but the lower your score, the more work you need to do. Below, list the problem areas you need to work on. For each problem area, describe one way to improve. Focus on one area for at least a week. When you have improved in that area, work on another. Continue until you think you have improved in all your problem areas. If you score is less than 48, you might want to meet with a teacher or counselor to discuss ways to improve your work qualities.

Ways to Become a More Valuable Employee

_____

_____

_____

_____

_____

_____

_____

_____

_____

_____

_____

_____

_____

_____

_____

_____

Topic 14
Strategies for a Positive Attitude

Discover

- the three components of work attitude.
- ten strategies for improving your work attitude.

Terms

opportunity

priority

self-confident

self-esteem

work attitude

work ethic

Key Concept

Focus on the positive.

Cases

- *Staying Positive*, page 90
- *Torn Between Two Priorities*, page 96

Reproducible Master

Self-Assessment: *Your Strategies for a Positive Attitude*, page T43

Activities

1. **Terms** Choose one of the vocabulary-building activities listed on page T8.
2. **Journal Writing** Your work attitude includes attitude toward self, work, and the workplace. Analyze your work attitude. If you do not work, use your attitude toward school instead.
3. **Journal Writing** Describe a difficult situation when you needed to maintain a positive attitude, even though it was difficult. What strategies did you use?
4. **Journal Writing** Describe how you could use each of the ten strategies to improve your attitude.
5. **Speaker** Invite one or more working people to discuss how they balance work life with personal life.

Topic 14, Self-Assessment

Your Strategies for a Positive Attitude

Name_____ **Date**_____ **Period**_____

Below is the list of ten strategies for a positive attitude. Apply these strategies to your life. For each strategy, give an example of how you have used or will use the strategy to maintain a positive attitude.

1. Examine your attitude regularly. _____
_____
_____

2. Balance your work and personal life. _____
_____
_____

3. Focus on the positive. _____
_____
_____

4. Communicate._____
_____
_____

5. Turn changes into opportunities. _____
_____
_____

6. Educate yourself. _____
_____
_____

7. Maintain interest._____
_____
_____

8. Maintain a sense of humor._____
_____
_____

9. Take care of your health._____
_____
_____

10. Dress for success. _____
_____
_____

Topic 15
Succeeding in a New Job

Discover

- techniques for making a smooth adjustment to a new job.
- why some jobs have a probation period for new workers.

Terms

employee handbook

orientation

performance review

probation

status quo

unwritten rules

written rules

Key Concept

Learn the written and unwritten rules of your workplace.

Cases

- *The Newest Worker*, page 98
- *A Difficult Adjustment*, page 102

Reproducible Master

Self-Assessment: *Can You Succeed in a New Job?*
page T45

Activities

1. **Terms** Choose one of the vocabulary-building activities listed on page T8.
2. **Journal Writing** Think of a time when you were a new person at a job, school, or club. What feelings did you experience? Were people friendly or distant? How did you react? What did you do to get to know people? What did people do to welcome you?
3. **Cooperative Learning** Organize students into small groups. Have each group identify the main categories to include in an employee handbook for an imaginary company.
4. **Research** Find a profile of a successful person. Write a report that answers the following questions: What traits does the person have? What strategies did he or she use to get through difficult times? What kind of attitude does the person have?
5. **Speaker** Find a person from the human resources department of a large company to speak to your class about the employee orientation process. Ask the speaker to share a portion of the presentation shown to new employees.

Topic 15, Self-Assessment

Can You Succeed in a New Job?

Name_____ Date_____ Period_____

Do you have the attitude you need to succeed in a new job? The following quiz can give you some insights. For each pair of statements, check the one that best describes you. Respond honestly.

A	Statement A	B	Statement B
	A. I am excited about meeting new people and learning new skills.		**B.** I am nervous about meeting new people and learning new skills.
	A. I am confident in my ability to adjust to a new situation.		**B.** I am fearful and insecure about my ability to adjust to a new situation.
	A. I realize it takes time to build effective working relationships.		**B.** I expect good relationships to happen quickly.
	A. I take satisfaction in doing my job well; feedback from others is nice but not necessary.		**B.** I need lots of praise and encouragement when I am working.
	A. I have little trouble asking questions and asking for help to understand new responsibilities		**B.** If I ask for help, I'm afraid people will think I'm stupid or incompetent.
	A. People usually like me. They think I am friendly and open.		**B.** I am naturally shy. People sometimes think I am snobbish or stuck up.
	A. I am quick to catch on to the unwritten rules in a situation.		**B.** I never seem to catch on to the unwritten rules of a situation.
	A. I accept constructive criticism and try to learn from it.		**B.** I am very sensitive; criticism hurts my feelings and makes me depressed.
	A. If coworkers are distant, I continue to act in a friendly manner toward them.		**B.** If coworkers are distant, I am distant toward them.
	A. I do my best from the moment I start my new job.		**B.** I figure that they will give me some slack for the first few weeks.
	Total A's:		**Total B's:**

(Continued)

Topic 15, Self-Assessment

Can You Succeed in a New Job? (*Continued*)

Name_____

Scoring

For each checkmark in the A column, give yourself one point. The checkmarks in the B column get no points.

My total score is _____.

Interpretation

Score	Meaning
9 or 10	Congratulations! Your attitude will help you adjust to a new job.
7 or 8	Your attitude is good.
5 or 6	Your attitude may interfere with your building good relationships on the job.
4 or less	Your attitude is poor. It may interfere with your relationships with coworkers and your success.

Action

It is always a good idea to work on improving your attitude; but the lower your score, the more work you need to do. Choose one of your B answers. Record it below. Then describe what you could do to improve your attitude. Work on improving this attitude for at least a week. When you have improved, choose another B answer, and repeat the process. If your score is 4 or less, you might want to meet with a teacher or counselor to discuss ways to improve your attitude.

B Answer: _____

_____

_____

Ways to Improve My Attitude: _____

_____

_____

_____

_____

_____

_____

_____

_____

_____

_____

_____

_____

_____

_____

Topic 16
Being a Reliable Employee

Discover

- the negative impact of being absent or tardy on the job.
- ways to avoid being tardy.

Terms

absenteeism

tardiness

unprofessional

Key Concept

Absenteeism and tardiness negatively affect your career.

Cases

- *Late Again*, page 104
- *Everyone Else Is Late*, page 108

Reproducible Master

Self-Assessment: *Are You a Reliable Employee?* page T48

Activities

1. **Terms** Choose one of the vocabulary-building activities listed on page T8.
2. **Journal Writing** What methods do you use to avoid being late to school, work, or other activities? Do these methods work? If not, what could you do to improve?
3. **Journal Writing** Do you consider yourself to be a reliable person? Explain by providing examples of your reliability.
4. **Cooperative Learning** Organize students into small groups. Have each group make a policy for an imaginary company that addresses employee tardiness and absenteeism. What should the penalties be for employees who arrive late or miss work without a good reason? What types of unscheduled absences would the company excuse? Have groups share their policies and discuss.
5. **Speaker** Invite a supervisor or manager to explain the importance of being at work and on time every day. The manager might also describe what action is taken at his or her workplace when someone is absent or late.

Topic 16, Self-Assessment

Are You a Reliable Employee?

Name_____ **Date**_____ **Period**_____

A reliable employee is never or rarely late or absent from work. Absenteeism and tardiness cost employers time, productivity, and money. Absenteeism and tardiness also cost the employee—in promotions, raises, good performance reviews, and the respect of supervisors and coworkers. Evaluate your own performance. Read each action, then place a check in the appropriate column for how often you behave in this way.

Action	Often	Sometimes	Rarely	Never
Ask others to cover for me.				
Fall behind in work due to absence.				
Late for appointments and meetings.				
Late for school/work on Mondays.				
Late for school/work every day.				
Late returning to school/work from lunch.				
Leave school/work early on Fridays.				
Make excuses for being late.				
Make excuses for not showing up.				
Miss deadlines for work or reports.				
Miss meetings or appointments.				
Miss school/work on Fridays.				
Miss school/work on Mondays.				
Take sick days when not sick.				
Totals:				

Scoring

Add the number of checkmarks in each column, and record in the last row.

Interpretation

A reliable employee would have most of his or her checkmarks in the "never" or "rarely" columns, with a very few in the "often" column. Imagine that you are in charge of hiring for your company. Look at your answers. Then answer the following questions.

1. Would you hire yourself, based on your answers? _____

2. Explain your answer._____

_____

_____

_____

_____

_____

_____

_____

_____

(Continued)

Topic 16, Self-Assessment

Are You a Reliable Employee? (*Continued*)

Name_____

Action

It is always a good idea to work on improving your reliability; but the more checks you had in "often" and "sometimes," the more work you need to do. Below, list the problem areas you need to work on. For each area, describe one way to improve. Focus on one area for at least a week. When you have improved in that area, work on another. Continue until you think you have improved in all your problem areas. If you had five or more checkmarks in "often" and "sometimes," you might want to meet with a teacher or counselor to discuss ways to improve your attendance problems.

How to Improve My Reliability

_____
_____
_____
_____
_____
_____
_____
_____
_____
_____
_____
_____
_____
_____
_____
_____
_____
_____
_____
_____
_____
_____
_____
_____
_____
_____

Topic 17
Career Plateaus

Discover

- how to stay positive when you hit a plateau.
- strategies for coping with work plateaus.

Terms

career plateau

career track

plateau

Key Concept

Stay positive during the ups and downs of career progress.

Cases

- *Changes in the Workplace*, page 110
- *Stuck on a Plateau*, page 114

Reproducible Master

Self-Assessment: *Are You Happy at Work?* page T51

Activities

1. **Terms** Choose one of the vocabulary-building activities listed on page T8.
2. **Journal Writing** Have you ever hit a plateau at school, work, or a hobby or sport? Describe the plateau. How did it develop? How long did it last? How did you feel? Did you do something to end the plateau? How did this experience affect your attitude toward future involvement in that endeavor?
3. **Cooperative Learning** Organize students into small groups. Have each group make a list of plateau experiences. For each one, have the group discuss if the plateau experience is good, bad, or neutral and what steps could be taken to get off the plateau and move forward.
4. **Research** Can a plateau period have value? Some plateaus enable growth or learning to become established before new growth or learning can take place. In chemistry, there is a temperature plateau when a substance changes phase from solid to liquid or liquid to gas. Have students research a plateau situation in human development or science.
5. **Speaker** Invite a school counselor to talk to students about plateaus in their school lives. What are some signs of a plateau involving school? How should students handle such a period?

Topic 17, Self-Assessment

Are You Happy at Work?

Name_____ **Date**_____ **Period** _____

When you are in a career plateau, it may be time to evaluate what you really want from a job. The following quiz will help you think about which factors at work are most important to you. Listed below are several factors that can affect your happiness at work. Rate how important each factor is to you. Use the following scale:

1 = very important, 2 = important, 3 = not important

Rating	Factor
	Being recognized for excellent work (A)
	Casual dress code (P)
	Free parking (P)
	Good benefits, such as health insurance, paid time off, flexible hours (P)
	Good location (P)
	Good management (R)
	Good reputation of the company (A)
	Good work hours (P)
	High wages or salary (A)
	Important job title (A)
	Job security (P)
	Nice supervisors (R)
	Opportunity to accomplish difficult tasks (A)
	Opportunity to advance (A)
	Opportunity to learn new skills (A)
	Parties and celebrations with coworkers (R)
	Pleasant coworkers (R)
	Pleasant working environment (P)
	Provide useful services to others (R)
	Working with people (R)
	Working without supervision (R)

(Continued)

Topic 17, Self-Assessment

Are You Happy at Work? (*Continued*)

Name_____

Scoring

Circle all the factors that you rated "1," very important. For each circled factor followed by a (P), place a check in the first column in the chart below. For each circled factor followed by (A), place a check in the second column. For each circle factor followed by (R), place a check in the last column. Count the number of checks in each column, and note the total on the bottom line of each column.

Physical Conditions (P)	Opportunities to Advance (A)	Relationships (R)
Total:	Total:	Total:

Interpretation

1. Based on the results in the chart above, which category of factors is most important to you?

   _____

   _____

2. Do you agree with the results in the chart? Explain your answer.

   _____

   _____

   _____

   _____

   _____

   _____

   _____

   _____

   _____

   _____

   _____

   _____

   _____

   _____

   _____

   _____

Topic 18
Planning Your Career Goals

Discover

- how to set goals to help you advance in your career.
- how to work smart to improve your chances of promotion.

Terms

ambition

network

professional organization

role model

Key Concept

Choose your goal, then develop a plan to reach it.

Cases

- *Working Smart*, page 116
- *Promoted over Your Friends*, page 120

Reproducible Master

Self-Assessment: *Set Your Career Goals*, page T54

Activities

1. **Terms** Choose one of the vocabulary-building activities listed on page T8.
2. **Journal Writing** Are you ambitious? What actions or thoughts support your answer?
3. **Journal Writing** Describe the person you view as a role model for career advancement. What important lessons can be drawn from that person's experiences?
4. **Journal Writing** Describe the type of career you want. Why do you think it suits your abilities, interests, and personality?
5. **Speaker** Invite a career counselor to talk with students about how to choose career goals and reach them.

Set Your Career Goals

Name_____ Date_____ Period_____

Successful people are often those who have set goals for themselves. What are your career goals? This activity will help you start discovering them.

1. Determine Your Interests

Analyze what you do best and what you most like to do. Think about all aspects of your life, for example, school, home, hobbies, clubs, friends, sports. Then for each area listed in the first column below, write in the second column your experiences that fit in that area.

Areas	My Experiences
Activities I most enjoy	
My best subjects in school	
Activities for which I have received awards	
Activities for which I have received recognition (includes positive comments by friends and teachers)	
My special skills, talents, and abilities	

2. Choose Five

Read over all the items you noted in the chart above. Which ones could you convert into a career goal? For example, if your best subject in school is math, you might be a math teacher or an accountant. On the lines below, list five possible career goals based on your chart.

_____

_____

_____

_____

_____

(Continued)

Topic 18, Self-Assessment

Set Your Career Goals (*Continued*)

Name_____

3. Set Your Career Goals

Based on the five career possibilities you listed, choose the one that appeals to you most right now. Write that career goal on the line below:

_____

Now you will develop short-term and long-term goals for achieving success in this career. A *short-term goal* is one that is to be achieved soon, within the next few weeks or months. Usually, short-term goals must be accomplished before the long-term goals can be started. A *long-term goal* is a goal that will take one or more years to achieve.

Time Frame	My Career Goals
Short-term	
Long-term	

Topic 19
Learning from Mistakes

Discover

- the positive side of making mistakes.
- strategies to use for dealing with mistakes.

Terms

perfectionist

Key Concept

Mistakes help you grow and can lead to success.

Cases

- *Budget Blues*, page 124
- *Oops!* page 128

Reproducible Master

Self-Assessment: *How Do You Handle Mistakes?*
  page T57

Activities

1. **Terms** Choose one of the vocabulary-building activities listed on page T8.
2. **Journal Writing** Describe a mistake you made that you will never forget. What did you do when you discovered it? What lesson did you learn from the experience?
3. **Cooperative Learning** Organize students into groups. Have each group make a list of mistakes. Then have the groups organize the mistakes into types, with a descriptive label for each and suggestions for them.
4. **Research** Many famous mistakes have been reported in the news and described in books. Choose a mistake from one of the following areas: business, engineering, food, medicine, military, and politics. Research the mistake and write a brief report about it. Describe what the mistake was, who committed it, the impact of the mistake, and what happened after the mistake was made.
5. **Speaker** Invite a manager to discuss what his or her company does to handle any mistakes made on the job.

Topic 19, Self-Assessment

How Do You Handle Mistakes?

Name_____ **Date**_____ **Period**_____

Everyone makes mistakes. The only people who never make mistakes are people who never try anything new. When you make a mistake, the best thing to do is admit it. Correct the mistake as soon as possible, and then determine what you need to do to keep from making the same mistake again. Answer the following questions based on your own experience.

1. What is the worst mistake you ever made? _____
   _____
   _____

2. How did you feel when you realized you made this mistake?_____
   _____
   _____

3. Did you admit your mistake promptly? If yes, did it help? If not, did it make matters worse? _____
   _____
   _____

4. Why do you think you made this mistake? _____
   _____
   _____

5. What did you learn from this mistake? _____
   _____
   _____

6. Did you use this mistake as a stepping-stone to new achievements? Explain. _____
   _____
   _____

7. Has fear of making a mistake ever prevented you from doing something? Explain. _____
   _____
   _____

8. If fear of making a mistake has kept you from doing something, what could you do to overcome this fear?_____
   _____
   _____

Topic 20
Repairing Relationships

Discover

- causes of damaged relationships.
- effective strategies to repair this damage.

Terms

common courtesy

competition

mutually rewarding relationship

personality conflict

Key Concept

Act promptly to restore damaged relationships.

Cases

- *The Misunderstanding*, page 130
- *Angry Words*, page 134

Reproducible Master

Self-Assessment: *How Do You Handle Human Relations Mistakes?* page T59

Activities

1. **Terms** Choose one of the vocabulary-building activities listed on page T8.
2. **Journal Writing** Do you think that any damaged relationship can be repaired, or are some too damaged to ever return to normal. Explain your answer.
3. **Cooperative Learning** Organize students into groups. Have each group make a list of common relationship problems among your peers. What are the leading causes of conflict? What steps could remedy many of these relationship problems?
4. **Cooperative Learning** Organize the students into groups. Have groups develop their own definition of *common courtesy* and describe three examples of common courtesy being shown. Then have them describe the same three situations, but with the opposite of common courtesy being shown. Have each group choose its best "opposite of common courtesy" situation, present it to the class, and have the class tell how common courtesy should be shown in that situation.
5. **Speaker** Invite a human resources professional, mediator, or social worker to speak to your class about avoiding personality conflicts and repairing damaged relationships.

How Do You Handle Human Relations Mistakes?

Name_____ Date_____ Period_____

Is your response to human relations mistakes causing you problems? The following quiz can give you some insight. Read each statement below. Check the "Agree" column if you agree. Check the "Disagree" column if you disagree.

Agree	Disagree	Statements
		1. When I have a conflict with another person, I am preoccupied with it; I replay the scene over and over in my mind.
		2. I analyze what people say to me, listening for slights or possible hidden insults.
		3. There are people I am unable to cooperate with because of personality conflicts.
		4. A major source of stress in my life arises from conflicts in my relationships with peers.
		5. A major source of stress in my life arises from my relationship with people who have authority over me.
		6. My personal productivity is sometimes affected by problems in my relationships with others.
		7. If someone makes a mistake, I have a hard time forgiving him or her; I dwell on it and expect it to happen again.
		8. If my relationship with someone has been damaged, I find it hard to make the first move to repair it.
		9. I tend to leap to conclusions about the motives of anyone who upsets or offends me.
		10. I have high standards for myself. If others do not measure up to my standards, I am not interested in building a relationship with them.

Scoring

Count the number of statements for which you checked the "Disagree" column. This number is your score.

My score is _____.

Interpretation

Score	Meaning
8 or more	Congratulations! You are doing a good job of repairing your relationships.
7 or less	You need to evaluate your attitude toward your own mistakes and the mistakes of others. Your negative attitude in this area is most likely interfering with your relationships and productivity.

(Continued)

Topic 20, Self-Assessment

How Do You Handle Human Relations Mistakes? (*Continued*)

Name_____

Action

Everyone can benefit by looking at the way a relationship has gone wrong. Below, describe one relationship problem. Then describe what you could have done to improve the situation. If you scored less than 8, you may have problems in the areas of oversensitivity and a negative attitude toward mistakes. You might want to meet with a teacher or counselor to discuss ways to improve your attitude toward mistakes and relationship problems.

Relationship Problem

_____
_____
_____
_____

What I Could Have Done to Improve the Situation

_____
_____
_____
_____
_____
_____
_____
_____
_____
_____
_____
_____
_____
_____
_____
_____
_____
_____
_____
_____
_____
_____

Topic 21
Dealing with Criticism

Discover

- why constructive criticism can help you succeed.
- how to give constructive criticism.

Terms

constructive criticism

criticism

defensive

destructive criticism

Key Concept

Accept criticism and learn from it.

Cases

- *The Troublemaker*, page 136
- *The New Supervisor*, page 140

Reproducible Master

Activity: *Giving Constructive Criticism*, page T62

Activities

1. **Terms** Choose one of the vocabulary-building activities listed on page T8.
2. **Journal Writing** Identify one situation in which you have benefited from criticism. Describe the situation, the criticism, and your response. Explain how you benefited.
3. **Journal Writing** How do you deal with criticism? Describe a situation in which someone criticized you. What caused the criticism? What did the person say? How was the message communicated and how did you respond? Do you think the criticism was appropriate?
4. **Journal Writing** Do you know anyone like Chen? Describe the ways in which this person is like Chen. How does this person make you and other people feel? What would you suggest to this person if you were giving him or her constructive criticism?
5. **Cooperative Learning** Organize students into small groups. Have students think about sports teams and how criticism is communicated to the members. What is the purpose of this criticism? How do players respond to it? What can you learn about criticism from observing sports teams?

Topic 21, Activity

Giving Constructive Criticism

Name_____ **Date**_____ **Period**_____

Which criticisms are constructive? Read the following statements. Place a check in the Yes column for the statements that are constructive. Place a check in the no column for the statements that are destructive. For all the No statements, rewrite them in the last column, so that they become constructive statements.

Constructive?		Statement	Rewrite "No's" To Be Constructive
Yes	No		
		1. "Late again? You haven't been on time once in the past three months."	
		2. "I think your report would be better if you expanded the section on inventory management."	
		3. "Are you sure these are the correct figures? Would you mind double-checking them for me?"	
		4. "Your questions are annoying me. Why can't you do it right the first time?"	
		5. "Just for once, I'd like to be able to delegate a job and have it done correctly."	
		6. "I can see you're having problems with this assignment. Let's go over it together."	
		7. "You seem out of it lately. If you can't keep your mind on the job, don't bother coming to work."	
		8. "I know you value your Individuality, but we do have a dress code. Here's a copy of it. I know with your sense of style you'll look good."	

Topic 22
Leaving a Job

Discover

- how to decide when it's time to leave a job.
- ways to leave a job in a positive manner.
- what to do if you are fired.

Terms

at-will employment

fired

giving notice

inertia

layoff

letter of resignation

reduction in force (rif)

resign

Key Concept

Analyze your reasons before you leave a job.

Cases

- *Ready to Move On?* page 142
- *Dealing with a Layoff*, page 146

Reproducible Master

Self-Assessment: *Résumé Planning*, page T64

Activities

1. **Terms** Choose one of the vocabulary-building activities listed on page T8.
2. **Journal Writing** Think of the groups or activities in which you participate, such as a course, club, team, or job. Have you ever had to leave one of them? If yes, describe how you left and whether the experience was positive. If no, describe how you would leave in a positive manner.
3. **Journal Writing** Have you ever experienced *inertia*? Describe the situation and why you were reluctant to make changes. How did you overcome your inertia?
4. **Research** Professional organizations are often an excellent way to learn about career paths and job opportunities. Choose a career that interests you, find one professional organization that serves that career, and write a brief report on the professional organization. Include information on how the organization helps members find jobs and advance in their careers.
5. **Speaker** Invite a career counselor to talk about pursuing career paths, knowing when you are ready to leave a job, and handling the transition.

Topic 22, Self-Assessment

Résumé Planning

Name_____ **Date**_____ **Period**_____

One of the most widely used tools in a job search is the résumé. The purpose of a résumé is to showcase the skills and abilities you offer an employer. A résumé should be one page long. In the résumé for your first job, you will probably emphasize school activities and volunteer experiences. After your first job, you will emphasize your work experiences.

To write a good résumé, first create a detailed list of your experiences, skills, and accomplishments. Use the chart below to list as many as possible. When you are done, read over your lists. Circle the items that would most impress a prospective employer. Highlight these on your résumé.

Educational Background	
Courses	
Awards	
Skills	

Work Experience	
Job 1 Description:	Job 2 Description:
Accomplishments	Accomplishments
Skills	Skills

Volunteer/Organizational Experience	
Organization 1:	Organization 2:
Awards	Awards
Skills	Skills